Written by: Joe Hill

Art by: Gabriel Rodriguez

Colors by: Jay Fotos

Letters by: Robbie Robbins

Series Edited by: Chris Ryall

Collection Edited by: Justin Eisinger

Collection Designed by: Robbie Robbins

JOE HILL:
to Owen & Naomi, with love.

- KEYS TO THE KINGDOM -

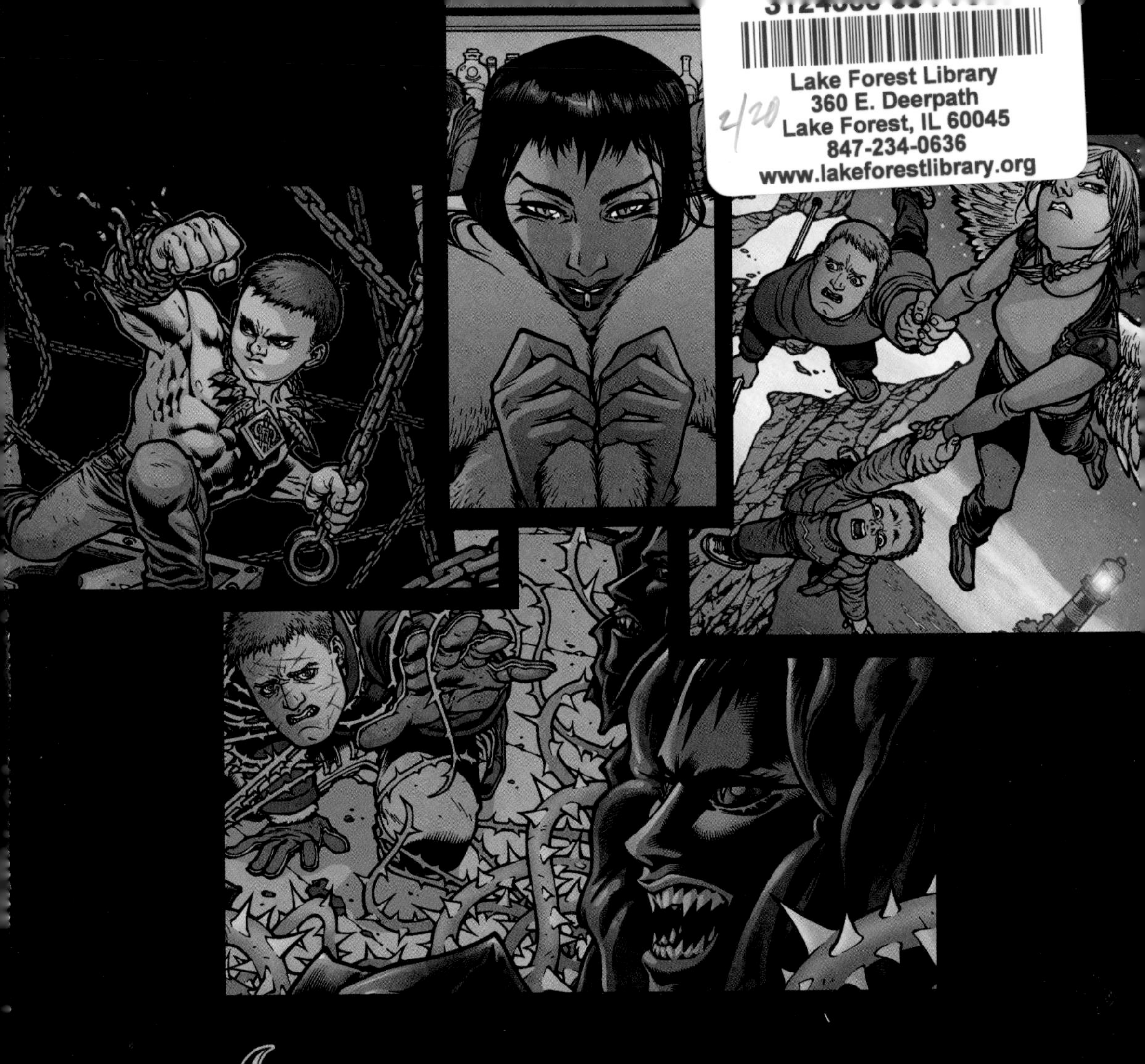

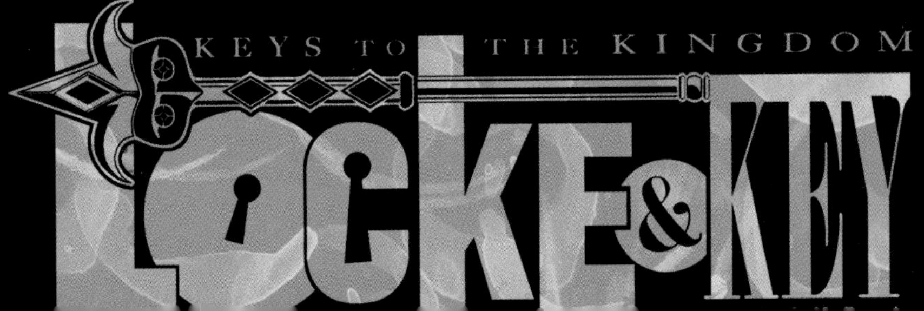
KEYS TO THE KINGDOM
LOCKE & KEY

Locke & Key created by Joe Hill and Gabriel Rodriguez

For international rights, contact licensing@idwpublishing.com

ISBN: 978-1-61377-207-2

22 21 20 19   9 10 11 12

- KEYS TO THE KINGDOM -

Chapter One

SPARROW

to Bill Watterson

I'M GLAD YOU COULD STOP BY FOR RECESS, MRS. LOCKE. I'M WORRIED ABOUT BODE'S ABILITY TO RELATE TO OTHER KIDS.
I'M SURPRISED HE'D BE HAVING TROUBLE MAKING FRIENDS. HE HAS SUCH A HUGE IMAGINATION.
WHAT'CHU DOING? MAKING A SNOW ANGEL?
I'M PRETENDING SOMEONE UNLOCKED MY HEAD, OPENED IT UP, AND TOOK OUT ALL MY THOUGHTS AND MEMORIES. NOW I'M SO COMPLETELY EMPTY-HEADED, I'VE LOST THE ABILITY TO THINK FOR MYSELF, TO STAND UP, OR EVEN TO CONTROL MY BODILY FUNCTIONS.
IT'S PROBABLY BEST FOR YOU ALL TO GO BEFORE I BEFOUL MYSELF.
C'MON. HIS FRICKIN' CASE OF WEIRD MIGHT BE CONTAGIOUS. LET'S GET THE WOLFPACK TOGETHER AND PLAY SOME FOOTBALL.
HE *DOES* HAVE A WONDERFUL VOCABULARY. SO FEW SEVEN-YEAR-OLDS CAN DROP THE WORD "BEFOUL" INTO CASUAL CONVERSATION.
I CAN SEE WHY YOU'RE WORRIED. I'LL TALK TO HIM.

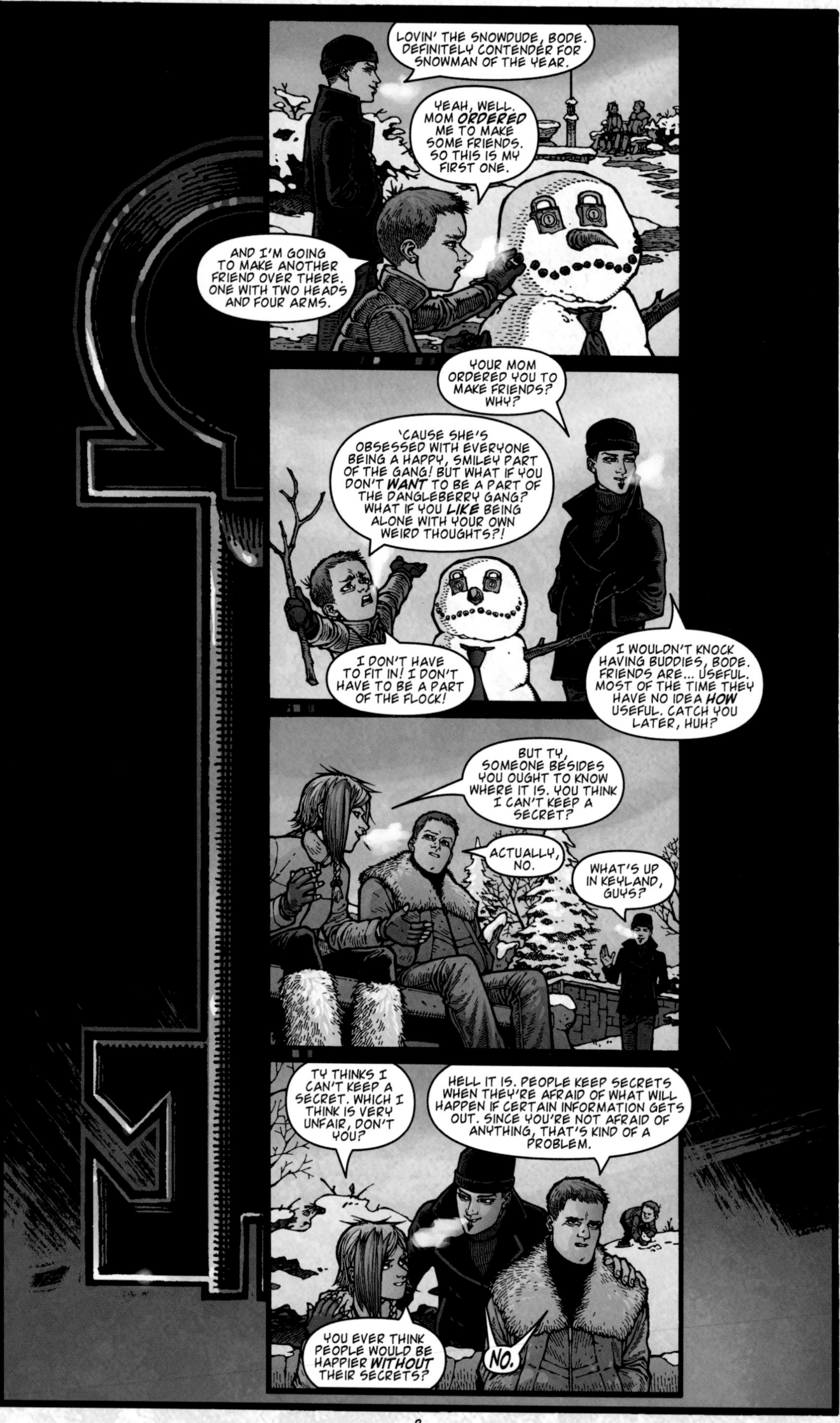
LOVIN' THE SNOWDUDE, BODE. DEFINITELY CONTENDER FOR SNOWMAN OF THE YEAR.
YEAH, WELL. MOM ORDERED ME TO MAKE SOME FRIENDS. SO THIS IS MY FIRST ONE.
AND I'M GOING TO MAKE ANOTHER FRIEND OVER THERE. ONE WITH TWO HEADS AND FOUR ARMS.
YOUR MOM ORDERED YOU TO MAKE FRIENDS? WHY?
'CAUSE SHE'S OBSESSED WITH EVERYONE BEING A HAPPY, SMILEY PART OF THE GANG! BUT WHAT IF YOU DON'T WANT TO BE A PART OF THE DANGLEBERRY GANG? WHAT IF YOU LIKE BEING ALONE WITH YOUR OWN WEIRD THOUGHTS?!
I DON'T HAVE TO FIT IN! I DON'T HAVE TO BE A PART OF THE FLOCK!
I WOULDN'T KNOCK HAVING BUDDIES, BODE. FRIENDS ARE... USEFUL. MOST OF THE TIME THEY HAVE NO IDEA HOW USEFUL. CATCH YOU LATER, HUH?
BUT TY, SOMEONE BESIDES YOU OUGHT TO KNOW WHERE IT IS. YOU THINK I CAN'T KEEP A SECRET?
ACTUALLY, NO.
WHAT'S UP IN KEYLAND, GUYS?
TY THINKS I CAN'T KEEP A SECRET. WHICH I THINK IS VERY UNFAIR, DON'T YOU?
HELL IT IS. PEOPLE KEEP SECRETS WHEN THEY'RE AFRAID OF WHAT WILL HAPPEN IF CERTAIN INFORMATION GETS OUT. SINCE YOU'RE NOT AFRAID OF ANYTHING, THAT'S KIND OF A PROBLEM.
YOU EVER THINK PEOPLE WOULD BE HAPPIER WITHOUT THEIR SECRETS?
NO.

CHUD
GOTCHA, ZACK. WUH-WANNA... UH... WANNA FIGHT?
YES. LET'S FIGHT.
GIVE IT. GIVE ME THE KEY TO THE BLACK DOOR OR THE WHORE DIES LIKE YOUR LITTLE FUCK BROTHER.
PLEASE. *PLEASE...*

BODE! YOU WANNA NOT ABSOLUTELY SOAK MY BOYFRIEND?!
SORRRR-EEEE. I THOUGHT...
WHOA. DID I JUST SAY WHAT I THINK I SAID?
UH–I DO THINK YOU JUST PROVED YOUR BROTHER'S POINT ABOUT HOW YOU'RE MAYBE NOT THE BEST SECRET-KEEPER OF ALL TIME. NO OFFENSE.
TY. HEY. I SHOULD'VE SAID SOMETHING, MAN. I'M SORRY.
DON'T APOLOGIZE TO HIM. THERE'S NOTHING TO APOLOGIZE FOR. C'MON, ZACK, LET'S GO. I CAN SEE TYLER'S GETTING READY TO BE A DICK.
...WE COULD ALL HAVE A BIG SNOWBALL...
WE SHOULD TALK ABOUT THIS.
LET'S NOT. I THINK I'M GOING TO HIT THE TRAILS FOR A WHILE.
BETTER THAN HITTING ME, I GUESS.
I HAVEN'T RULED THAT OUT YET.
@#$%! TEENAGERS! WHAT THE HECK IS WRONG WITH THEM?!
JUST WHEN YOU'RE ABOUT TO GET A GOOD SNOWBALL FIGHT GOING, THEY HAVE TO RUIN IT BY TALKING ABOUT RELATIONSHIPS!

LIKE ALL BUDDING MALES, TESTOSTERONE SURGES THROUGH MY BLOOD, COMPELLING ME TO COMMIT WANTON ACTS OF BRUTALITY TO THE MOST INNOCENT CREATURES.
IT'S SOMETHING YOU CAN NEVER KNOW, PITIFUL SPARROW--THE SAVAGE THRILL OF CORNERING A WEAK, VULNERABLE, AND BASICALLY STUPID, ANIMAL WHEN IT'S ALL ALONE.
OKAY. POINT MADE.
SHREE. SHREE.
SCIENTISTS NEVER STUDY THE IMPORTANT THINGS. LIKE WHY SOME ANIMALS APPEAR TO HAVE EVOLVED THE ABILITY TO GLOAT.

FIVE MINUTES AGO, WE WERE FRIENDS. NOW HE THINKS I'M LIKE—
A WOLF IN SHEEP'S CLOTHING? FORGET IT. YOU'RE STILL FRIENDS AND HE'LL GET OVER IT. HE WAS GOING TO FIND OUT SOMETIME.
LOOK AT THE SILVER LINING. NO MORE SECRETS. WE CAN BE OUT IN THE OPEN NOW. LIKE IF TYLER WAS STANDING RIGHT HERE WE COULD JUST—
MAYBE YOU'RE RIGHT. MAYBE SECRETS ARE ALWAYS A MISTAKE. LIKE... WHAT WERE YOU AND TY TALKING ABOUT WHEN I WALKED UP? SOUNDED LIKE TY HAS SOME KEY HE ISN'T SHARING.
YOU DON'T WANT TO KNOW ABOUT IT. NOT THIS ONE.
I WISH I HAD TIME TO GO AFTER TYLER. I'D LIKE TO TALK TO HIM, BUT I PROMISED AUNT ELLIE I'D BE HOME EARLY TO HELP WITH RUFUS. IF I DON'T SHOW UP, I'LL BE IN THE DOGHOUSE ALL WEEK.
I'LL HUNT TYLER DOWN. GO ON. TAKE CARE OF WHAT YOU GOT TO TAKE CARE OF.
THANKS. THINK I WILL.

TY! TYLER! HEY!
YOU'RE SO PREDICTABLE. I KNEW YOU'D BE PISSED WHEN YOU—
I'M PREDICTABLE? HAVE I EVER HAD A FRIEND YOU *DIDN'T* WANT TO CLIMB ALL OVER?
I DON'T HAVE TO CLEAR MY BOYFRIENDS WITH YOU. JESUS, WHO THE HELL DIED AND GAVE YOU THE KEYS TO THE CHASTITY BELT?
DAD.
HE'S WHO DIED. REMEMBER HIM? YOU REMEMBER ME AND DAD WERE BARELY *TALKING* TO EACH OTHER WHEN HE GOT KILLED? YOU KNOW *WHY*? YOU HAVE ANY IDEA? DO YOU HAVE ANY FUCKING CLUE HOW MUCH OF THIS—*ALL OF IT*—IS MY FAULT?
TY. HEY. *HEY.*
NONE OF THIS IS YOUR FAULT. HOW CAN YOU EVEN THINK THAT?

I UNDERSTAND ALREADY. ONE TURN OF THE ANIMAL KEY, AND I WILL UNLOCK THE BEAST WITHIN, TRANSFORMING INTO MY SECRET ANIMAL SELF.
SOON THE FORESTS OF LOVECRAFT WILL SHUDDER AT THE FEARSOME HOWL OF THE SILVERBACK GORILLA!
UNLESS MY TRUE ESSENCE TAKES THE FORM OF A SLAVERING, COLD-BLOODED CROCODILE, WHO WILL CLAMBER FROM THE SEWERS OF LOVECRAFT, TO SPREAD PANIC WITH EACH SNAP OF HIS VISE-LIKE JAWS!
GREAT. THAT'S JUST GREAT. HOW AM I SUPPOSED TO INSPIRE FEAR AND DREAD LIKE THIS?
I GUESS I COULD POOP ON SOMEONE.

THE SKIES BELONG TO ME!
I CLAIM POSSESSION OF THE BLUE AERIAL SEA WITH ITS SHIMMERING CURRENTS OF SUNLIGHT!
I AM SOLE EMPEROR OF ALL I SURVEY!
I STAND ALONE, MARKED OUT BY THIS UNIVERSE TO DOMINATE THE VAST WORLD THAT LIES ABOVE THE HEADS OF MEN, THE RUGGEDLY INDEPENDENT HERO OF AN EPIC WRITTEN IN THE CLOUDS!
I—*EXCUSE* ME—HELLO—WOULD YOU MIND—*UNF!*
IT'S AMAZING HOW MUCH LESS RUGGEDLY INDEPENDENT YOU FEEL WHEN YOU'VE GOT A BEAK FULL OF SOMEONE'S ASS FEATHERS.

AUUAAAAAOOOOOOO
WHAT THE HELL IS THAT?
BEATS ME. LON CHANEY?

I REALLY AM SORRY, TY. I MEAN, I'M NOT SORRY THAT I'M WITH ZACK. BUT I AM THAT I DIDN'T FIND A CLASSY WAY TO TELL YOU.
AT LEAST HE'S A GOOD GUY. I HOPE YOU'LL REMEMBER THAT AND NOT DECIDE, JUST 'CAUSE WE'RE GOING OUT, THAT HE'S LIKE A TOTAL MASS MURDERER OR SOMETHING.
WHEREAS I'M NOT SO SURE WE CAN SAY THAT ABOUT YOUR GIRLFRIEND.

WHAT ARE WE DOING?
GOING THIS WAY!
THIS WAY!
THIS WAY!
GOING THIS WAY!
WHAT ARE WE DOING NOW?
GOING THIS WAY!
THIS WAY!
THIS WAY!
GOING THIS WAY!
AND NOW WE GO UP! I SEE THE PATTERN! THE GLORIOUS BEAUTIFUL PATTERN! I AM ONE WITH THE FLOCK!
I UNDERSTAND!
OUCHIE.
I DON'T UNDERSTAND.

SO WHO DECIDES WHAT DIRECTION TO FLY?
ME!
ME!
ME!
OH, COME ON. SOMEONE HAS TO BE IN CHARGE.
SOMEONE HAS TO BE TOP DOG, BIG MAN, THE PREZ.
YOU CAN'T ALL BE EQUALLY IMPORTANT, OF EQUAL VALUE, AND HAVE EQUAL SAY. THAT'S MADNESS! THAT'S CHAOS! THAT'S... THAT'S—
SHARING!
SHARING!
SHARING!
SHARING!
I KNOW MAN IS THE SUPERIOR SPECIES.
I JUST CAN'T REMEMBER EXACTLY WHY.

I'D ASK WHAT YOU SEE IN JORDAN, BUT SINCE YOU NEVER TAKE YOUR EYES OFF HER ASS—
IT ISN'T JUST THAT. I MEAN, SHE IS THE MOST BEAUTIFUL GIRL WHO'S EVER ACTUALLY TALKED TO ME. BUT IT'S SOMETHING ELSE TOO.
I'VE HEARD STORIES ABOUT HER. SHE'S BEEN KNOCKED AROUND SOME. IF SHE GETS ANGRY, IT'S ONLY 'CAUSE SHE'S AFRAID OF TRUSTING PEOPLE. I FEEL LIKE—SOMEHOW— IF I COULD HELP HER A LITTLE—IF I COULD FIX...
WHAT, YOU'RE GOING TO FIX HER? FIRST YOU TELL ME EVERYTHING'S YOUR FAULT, THEN YOU SAY YOU'RE GOING TO FIX THIS GIRL. IF YOU COULD GET OUTSIDE YOUR OWN HEAD FOR A MINUTE, I THINK—TY!
AA!
GNNNNNNNN.
FUCK YOU WANT?
WHAT DO YOU MEAN, WHAT DO THEY WANT? THEY WANT DINNER.
I DON'T KNOW ABOUT THAT.

SSSSSSSSSTTT
YEAH. I KIND OF THOUGHT THAT WAS WHAT YOU WERE AFTER. FORGET ABOUT IT, BITCH.
TYLER, WHO ARE YOU—
IT'S HER. IT'S THE DARK LADY. DAMN, EVERY TIME SHE TAKES A NEW FORM SHE GETS UGLIER.
HEY, TY, YOU KNOW JACKIE VEDA SET A NEW SCHOOL RECORD IN THE 500 THIS YEAR? LAST RACE OF THE SEASON.
AWESOME. I'LL BE SURE AND CONGRATULATE HER IF WE AREN'T TORN TO SHREDS. I NEED TO KNOW THIS—*WHY*?
'CAUSE I WAS LESS THAN A SECOND BEHIND HER WHEN SHE DID IT.
TRY AND KEEP UP.

HEY! MY BROTHER AND SISTER ARE IN TROUBLE!
WHAT DO WE DO?
GUYS! GUYS! MY FAMILY IS IN DANGER! THEY'RE BEING CHASED BY WILD DOGS! WHAT DO WE DO?
WHAT DO WE DO?
SAVE THEM!
SAVE THEM!
ATTACK FORMATION!
NICE! WHAT'S OUR PLAN?
SOME OF US WILL PITIFULLY THROW OUR BODIES INTO THEIR OPEN JAWS AND HOPE THE DOGS CHOKE ON OUR CORPSES!
THE OTHERS WILL SHRIEK FOR ALL THEY'RE WORTH IN AN ATTEMPT TO GIVE THE ATTACKERS CRIPPLING MIGRAINES!
I'M SO, SO, SO SORRY I ASKED.

STOP RIGHT THERE OR I'LL–
SCHWACK
NOOOO!
FALL DEAD IN A MESS OF BLOOD AND FEATHERS?
THIS IS THE RULE OF FANG AND PAW. THE ONLY REASON FOR YOUR EXISTENCE IS TO PROVIDE SUPERIOR ANIMALS LIKE MYSELF WITH A SNACK BETWEEN BIGGER MEALS.
THAT'S HOW IT IS WHEN NATURE DOESN'T GIVE YOU A SINGLE WEAPON TO DEFEND YOURSELVES. FACE IT–YOU'VE GOT NOTHING.
YOU'RE WRONG.
OH, YEAH? WHAT DO YOU GOT?
FRIENDS.

SHREEE SHREEE SHREEE SHREEE
TY!
KEEP GOING!
SHREEE SHREEE SHREEE SHREEE
SNNNNNGGGG...
UNGH. GET THE FUCK OUTTA MY FACE YOU UGLY—
—BITCH? HEY. HEY.
SHREEE SHREEE SHREEE SHREEE
AAAARRRK!
SHREEE SHREEE SHREEE SHREEE

SHREEE SHREEE SHREEE SHREEE
SHREEE SHREEE SHREEE SHREEE
SHREEE SHREEE SHREEE SHREEE
SHREEE SHREEE SHREEE SHREEE

BODE?
BODE?

WHAT'CHU DOIN'? BET IT'S SOMETHING WEIRD.
I'M BEING A SPARROW.
DID I CALL THAT, OR WHAT? C'MON... WOLFPACK UP, GUYS. IT'S SMASH TIME.
AREN'T YOU GOING WITH THEM?
NAW. SMASH TIME IS ONLY FUN IF YOU'RE THE ONE DOING THE SMASHING. ANYWAY. THEY SAY I CAN'T BE A WOLF BECAUSE OF MY NAME.
WHAT'S YOUR NAME?
BIRD. JASON BIRD. ONLY, YOU KNOW... EVERYONE CALLS ME JAY BIRD.
REALLY? THAT IS SORT OF A FUNNY NAME.
LOOK WHO'S TALKING. BODE LOCKE. SOUNDS LIKE SOMETHING I'D PUT ON MY BIKE TO KEEP IT FROM GETTING STOLEN.
YEAH. GOOD POINT. SO. YOU WANNA PLAY MY WEIRD GAME?

- KEYS TO THE KINGDOM -

Chapter Two

WHITE

HOW DOES A FUCKIN' HALFRICAN WHO WENT TO A CHURCH SAYIN' 9-11 WAS VENGEANCE ON THE WHITE MAN, HOW DOES THAT GUY WIND UP TELLIN' ME I GOT TO PAY FOR SOMEONE ELSE'S HEALTH CARE?
I JUST SAID HE COULD PLAY BASKETBALL. I WAS WATCHIN' HIM ON TV. HE GOT A GOOD MOVE TO THE LEFT.
THEY CAN ALL PLAY BASKETBALL. WHY I DON'T WATCH THAT SHIT ANYMORE. IT'S DISCRIMINATORY FOR NORMAL WHITE PEOPLE.

I CAN'T HARDLY GET A WHEELCHAIR THROUGH. WERE YOU ALL GOING TO FINISH WITH THIS WALK?
MA'AM, YES, MA'AM. BEAUTIFUL DAY TO SHOVEL FOR MINIMUM WAGE, ISN'T IT, MIZ BLAXTON?
BRIXTON, MR. PARSONS. IF YOU HAVE TROUBLE READING MY NAME TAG, YOU SHOULD POKE YOUR HEAD IN THE CONTINUING EDUCATION OFFICE. THEY OFFER DISCOUNTS FOR STAFF ON PRIVATE MENTORING.

CONGRATS ON ANOTHER WIN. TOO BAD FENCING IS SUCH A WEENIE SPORT. IT'S EVEN MORE DINKY THAN LACROSSE AND ROUGHLY AS COOL AS BEING IN THE WORLD OF WARCRAFT CLUB.
I THINK IT'S COOL.
HER APPROVAL ACTUALLY SUPPORTS MY ARGUMENT.

DON'T LISTEN TO TYLER, ZACK. HE'S JUST JEALOUS. CHICKS DIG FENCING.
IT'S SUCH A TURN-ON, WATCHING A BUNCH OF GUYS DRESSED LIKE MARSHMALLOW MEN, WEARING CODPIECES AND, UM, STABBING THEIR BIG, LONG POKERS INTO EACH OTHER. **AHUM.**
AND WHEN YOU ACHIEVE PENETRATION —*AHHEH-HUM!*— IT'S JUST—JUST SO— *AHEH-HEH HAAA-HAAAA*— I'M SORRY...

I DON'T GET IT. I'M UNDEFEATED THIS SEASON, AND TYLER'S HOCKEY TEAM HASN'T WON A SINGLE GAME. HOW DOES THAT MAKE **ME** THE PUNCHLINE?
I MEAN— *UNH?*
DDDDAA **AAUUUU—**
—AAAUUUUGE! *RENDELLLLL! DODGE! DODGE!*

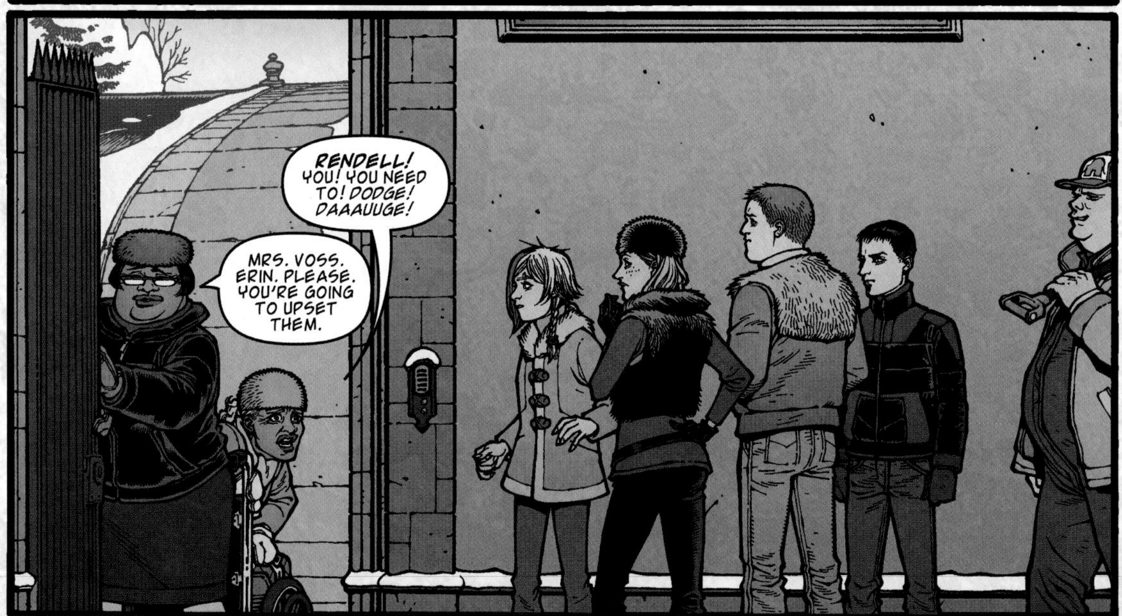
RENDELL! YOU! YOU NEED TO! *DODGE! DAAAUUGE!*
MRS. VOSS. ERIN. PLEASE. YOU'RE GOING TO UPSET THEM.

MRS. VOSS. ERIN VOSS? MY NAME IS KINSEY LOCKE. MY FATHER WAS RENDELL.
YOU TWO KNEW EACH OTHER, DIDN'T YOU? YOU WERE FRIENDS. YOU WENT DOWN IN THE CAVES TOGETHER. DO YOU REMEMBER KEYHOUSE? DO YOU REMEMBER—
NO! WHITE! WHITE!
WHITE!
YOU ALL WANT TO LEAVE THIS WOMAN BE, NOW.
WHY IS SHE SCARED OF ME? WHAT DID I DO?
AW, DON'T TAKE IT PERSONAL, DARLING. SHE'S GOT A MENTAL DEFORMITY. UNNATURALLY PREJUDICED AGAINST WHITE PEOPLE. GOES WITH THE TERRITORY. EVERYONE'S GOT SUMMIN IN THIS JOINT.
WHAT JOINT?
S'ON THE SIGN.

McCLELLAN PSYCHIATRIC HOSPITAL
TYLER. THAT WOMAN. SHE MIGHT KNOW SOMETHING ABOUT DAD. AND KEYHOUSE. AND... AND...
AND NOTHING. LET IT GO.
LET IT *GO?* WHAT ARE YOU THINKING?
I'M THINKING SHIT IS ALMOST NORMAL FOR ONCE AND I KIND OF LIKE IT. I'M THINKING I'VE ALREADY HAD ENOUGH CRAZY IN MY LIFE.
TYLER. WE CAN'T WALK AWAY FROM THIS.
WATCH ME.
YOU PLAY NANCY DREW IF YOU HAVE TO. JUST DEAL ME OUT.

I NEED TO GET IN THERE. I NEED TO TALK TO HER.

WHY? I MEAN, YES, SHE KNEW YOUR FATHER, THAT SEEMS EVIDENT. BUT—
SHE DIDN'T JUST KNOW HIM. THEY WERE FRIENDS. BEST FRIENDS.

YOU CAN'T KNOW THAT. DID YOUR DAD EVER SAY ANYTHING ABOUT ERIN VOSS TO YOU?
DIDN'T NEED TO.
"SHE WAS ON THE WALL. DOWN IN THE DROWNING CAVE."
ERIN VOS

BY THE TIME WE GOT OUT OF THE CAVE, I HAD MOSTLY FORGOTTEN ABOUT WHAT WAS ON THE WALL. GOT A LITTLE DISTRACTED TRYING NOT TO DROWN.
BUT WHEN HER NURSE SAID HER NAME, IT ALL CAME BACK TO ME.

I GUESS I STILL DON'T GET WHY YOU WANT TO TALK TO HER. I MEAN, EVEN IF SHE WAS CLOSE TO YOUR FATHER IN HIGH SCHOOL... WHAT COULD SHE POSSIBLY TELL YOU THAT YOU NEED TO KNOW ABOUT?
MY DAD DIDN'T TALK MUCH ABOUT GOING TO LOVECRAFT ACADEMY. I ALWAYS THOUGHT IT WAS BECAUSE HIS MOTHER DIED WHEN HE WAS IN HIGH SCHOOL AND HE WAS SAD ABOUT IT.
BUT THERE WAS SOMETHING ELSE. I KNOW THERE WAS SOMETHING ELSE. AND I THINK THIS ERIN VOSS MIGHT BE ABLE TO TELL ME WHAT.
EVEN IF SHE DOES KNOW SOMETHING, AND YOU COULD GET IN THERE, DOESN'T SOUND LIKE SHE'D WANT TO SHARE IT WITH YOU...
...WHITEY.
THAT WAS THE WORST PART. SHE COULDN'T HANDLE THE SIGHT OF US. SHE LOOKED AT US AND SAW A LYNCH MOB.
IN HER MIND WE WERE... CRIMINALS— WE WERE DANGEROUS— JUST 'CAUSE OF THE COLOR OF OUR SKIN. HOW SCREWED UP IS THAT?
THERE ARE SO MANY IRONIC STATEMENTS I COULD INSERT INTO THE CONVERSATION AT THIS POINT, I CAN'T CHOOSE BETWEEN THEM.
NOW WAIT A MINUTE THERE, MATE. YOU'RE TALKING ABOUT RACISM. THE PROBLEM WITH THE DAME IN McCLELLAN IS THAT SHE'S COMPLETELY MENTAL.
I RATHER THINK ONE THING IS DIFFERENT FROM THE OTHER.
SURE, IT'S DIFFERENT. 'CAUSE THE SHOE IS ON THE OTHER FOOT.
WHITE PEOPLE AREN'T USED TO DUDES MAKING BROAD, SWEEPING GENERALIZATIONS ABOUT THEM. THEY'RE MORE COMFORTABLE BEING THE ONES WHO GENERALIZE. THE MAJORITY ALWAYS IS.
I KIND OF WALKED INTO THIS ONE, HUH?
STILL. IT'S FUNNY TO THINK ERIN VOSS USED TO BE FRIENDS WITH MY DAD— WHO WAS SO WHITE HE'D SING ALONG TO PETER CETERA—AND NOW THE SIGHT OF WHITE PEOPLE IS ENOUGH TO KICK OFF A SCREAMING FIT.
I HAVE TO GET IN THERE. EITHER OF YOU HAVE ANY IDEA WHERE I CAN GET A GRAPPLING HOOK AND SOME ROPE?
YOU CAN SKIP THAT. IT'S NOT EXACTLY A HIGH-SECURITY INSTALLATION. MY UNCLE USED TO WORK THERE.
NO SHIT? LIKE AS WHAT? JANITOR OR SOMETHING?

YOU'RE SO SIMPLE. YOU JUST LIKE TO STICK YOUR DICK IN THINGS AND GENTLY STIR.
MY UNCLE WAS A PAYROLL ACCOUNTANT—SHITHEAD—BACK WHEN IT WAS STILL A GOOD GIG.
BUT IT'S A LOUSY NEIGHBORHOOD. THAT WHOLE AREA IS OLD AND WHITE AND IRISH AND BROKE AND ANGRY. PEOPLE DRIVING AROUND WITH BUMPER STICKERS THAT SAY "SOMEWHERE IN AFRICA, A VILLAGE IS MISSING ITS IDIOT."

SECOND TIME SOMEONE SCRATCHED "NIGGER" ON THE HOOD OF MY UNCLE'S OLDS, HE SAID "GOOD ENOUGH" AND CALLED IT QUITS.
PEOPLE SUCK.
WHEN HE STILL WORKED THERE, THOUGH, HE USED TO HAVE ME OVER SATURDAY NIGHTS TO VOLUNTEER. KIDS COME BY TO READ BOOKS TO THE OLDER FOLKS. IF YOU'VE GOT A COPY OF BELOVED IN YOUR HAND, YOU CAN WALTZ RIGHT IN.
ALL RIGHT. SATURDAY, THEN.
BUT KINSEY, LUV—EVEN IF YOU GET IN, SO WHAT? YOU ALREADY KNOW SHE ISN'T GOING TO TALK TO YOU. LOOK IN THE MIRROR...

...YOU'RE STILL WHITE.

TAVERN
THE FUCK YOU TALKING ABOUT? LEATHERFACE WOULD KICK THE SHIT OUT OF FREDDY KRUEGER. IT'S UNREALISTIC TO EVEN IMAGINE IT'D BE A FIGHT.
THE CHAINSAW GUY HAS 150 POUNDS ON ROBERT ENGLUND, EASY. NOW I'M A BIG MOTHERFUCKER. I DON'T CARE IF A GUY DOES HAVE KNIVES FOR FINGERS. NOT GOOD ENOUGH.
YOU PUT ME IN A RING WITH SOME WHIPPY-THIN BITCH LIKE FREDDY, I DON'T CARE IF HE'S GOT A FISTFUL OF KNIVES. LET HIM POKE ME A COUPLE TIMES. I'LL TAKE HIS LITTLE STICKERS AWAY AND KNIFE-FUCK HIM IN THE ASS.
HAVE YOU EVER EVEN SEEN ANY OF THESE MOVIES? LIKE, FREDDY—HE'S MADE OUT OF BAD DREAMS. HE'D COME OUT OF NOWHERE AND YANK YOU INTO HIS NIGHTMARE WORLD WHEN YOU LEAST EXPECT IT.
WHAT ARE YOU TALKIN ABOUT, YANK ME INTO THE NIGHTMARE WORLD?
I ALREADY MOP THE FLOORS THERE. MY WHOLE SHITTY LIFE IS ONE BIG, LONG, UNDERPAID BAD DREAM, PULLIN' WEEKEND SHIFTS IN McCLELLAN, SURROUNDED BY PANTS-SHITTING LUNATICS AND TAKIN' ORDERS FROM SMART-MOUTH, OVEREDUCATED NIG—
McCLELLAN. YOU WORK THERE, DON'T YOU?
HEL—LO THERE.
UNNNH... WHAT'D YOU SAY?
McCLELLAN HOSPITAL. I NOTICED YOUR OUTFITS WHEN I CAME IN.

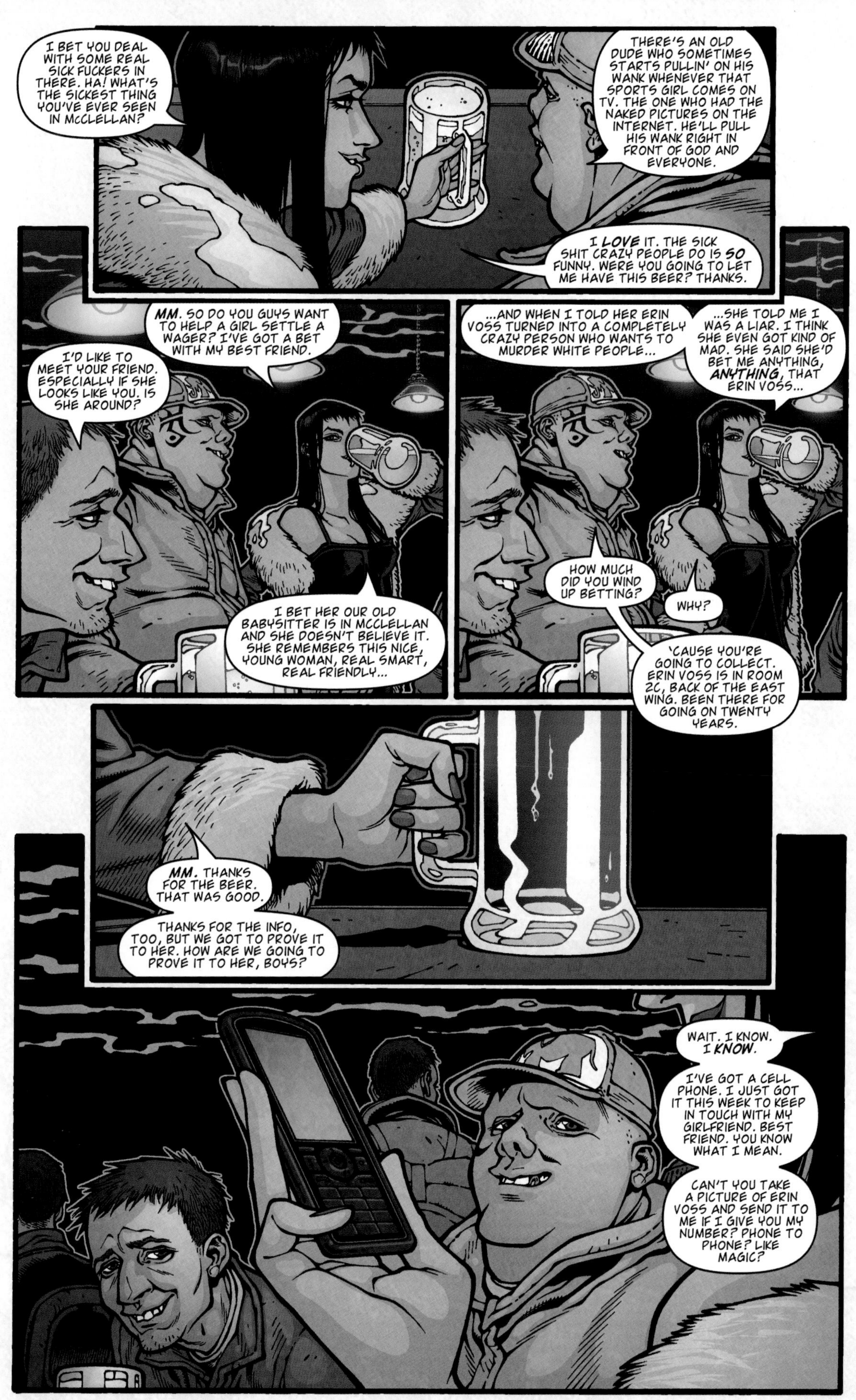
I BET YOU DEAL WITH SOME REAL SICK FUCKERS IN THERE. HA! WHAT'S THE SICKEST THING YOU'VE EVER SEEN IN McCLELLAN?
THERE'S AN OLD DUDE WHO SOMETIMES STARTS PULLIN' ON HIS WANK WHENEVER THAT SPORTS GIRL COMES ON TV. THE ONE WHO HAD THE NAKED PICTURES ON THE INTERNET. HE'LL PULL HIS WANK RIGHT IN FRONT OF GOD AND EVERYONE.
I LOVE IT. THE SICK SHIT CRAZY PEOPLE DO IS SO FUNNY. WERE YOU GOING TO LET ME HAVE THIS BEER? THANKS.
MM. SO DO YOU GUYS WANT TO HELP A GIRL SETTLE A WAGER? I'VE GOT A BET WITH MY BEST FRIEND.
I'D LIKE TO MEET YOUR FRIEND. ESPECIALLY IF SHE LOOKS LIKE YOU. IS SHE AROUND?
I BET HER OUR OLD BABYSITTER IS IN McCLELLAN AND SHE DOESN'T BELIEVE IT. SHE REMEMBERS THIS NICE, YOUNG WOMAN, REAL SMART, REAL FRIENDLY...
...AND WHEN I TOLD HER ERIN VOSS TURNED INTO A COMPLETELY CRAZY PERSON WHO WANTS TO MURDER WHITE PEOPLE...
...SHE TOLD ME I WAS A LIAR. I THINK SHE EVEN GOT KIND OF MAD. SHE SAID SHE'D BET ME ANYTHING, ANYTHING, THAT ERIN VOSS...
HOW MUCH DID YOU WIND UP BETTING?
WHY?
'CAUSE YOU'RE GOING TO COLLECT. ERIN VOSS IS IN ROOM 2C, BACK OF THE EAST WING. BEEN THERE FOR GOING ON TWENTY YEARS.
MM. THANKS FOR THE BEER. THAT WAS GOOD.
THANKS FOR THE INFO, TOO, BUT WE GOT TO PROVE IT TO HER. HOW ARE WE GOING TO PROVE IT TO HER, BOYS?
WAIT. I KNOW. I KNOW.
I'VE GOT A CELL PHONE. I JUST GOT IT THIS WEEK TO KEEP IN TOUCH WITH MY GIRLFRIEND. BEST FRIEND. YOU KNOW WHAT I MEAN.
CAN'T YOU TAKE A PICTURE OF ERIN VOSS AND SEND IT TO ME IF I GIVE YOU MY NUMBER? PHONE TO PHONE? LIKE MAGIC?

LIKE MAGIC THAT'S BEEN AROUND SINCE 1997. DO I GET A PICTURE IN RETURN?
PICTURE OF WHAT?
HOW ABOUT A PICTURE OF YOUR TITS? I BETTER GET SOMETHING GOOD. I COULD GET SHITCANNED, TAKIN' SNAPS OF THE PATIENTS.

I'LL DO YOU BETTER THAN SEND YOU A PIC. YOU SEND THE PHOTO I WANT, WE'LL GET TOGETHER AGAIN AND I'LL LET YOU FEEL THE GOODIES.
UNNH. FEEL THE—OH, FUCK YOU. YOU'RE PULLING MY CHAIN. WHO PUT YOU UP TO THIS?
I'M NOT PULLING YOUR CHAIN NOW, BUT YOU DO THIS FOR ME, AND WE WILL GET UP CLOSE AND PERSONAL. I PROMISE.

OH, HEY. YOU CAN'T JUST SEND ME A PICTURE OF THE OLD LADY IN BED. I NEED TO SEE THE DOOR INTO HER ROOM, TOO. MAKE SURE THE PICTURE SHOWS THE DOOR. CAN YOU DO THAT?

WHY... WHY WOULD YOU...

TO PROVE YOU TOOK THE PHOTO IN McCLELLAN—THAT SHE'S REALLY IN A HOSPITAL ROOM. SILLY. HERE'S MY NUMBER.

I CAN GET A PICTURE OF THE DOOR, THE HALL OUTSIDE, THE WHOLE FRICKIN' ROOM, NO PROBLEM. MY NEXT SHIFT IS SAD'DAY AFTERNOON. LOOK FOR SOMETHING ON YOUR CELL THEN.

AREN'T THEY COOL? CELL PHONES? THE INTERNET, E-MAIL, iPODS... THE 21ST CENTURY IS GNARLY.

I MEAN, REALLY. FUCK THE '80S. I LOVE IT HERE.

WHAT?

IF I FIX IT SO YOU CAN TALK TO HER, YOU HAVE TO GIVE ME BACK THE HEAD KEY AND YOU HAVE TO TAKE ME WITH YOU AND YOU HAVE TO INCLUDE ME WHEN YOU MAKE PLANS, FROM NOW ON, FOREVER.
WHAT ARE YOU TALKING ABOUT? WHEN WE MAKE PLANS? WHAT DO YOU HAVE BEHIND YOUR BACK?

YOU AND TYLER. WHEN YOU TALK ABOUT THE HOUSE AND THE CAVE AND THE OMEGA KEY AND THE BAD LADY, YOU DON'T EVER INCLUDE ME BECAUSE YOU THINK I'M SCARED BUT I'M NOT SCARED I WANT TO BE PART OF IT AND THAT'S THE DEAL.
HOW ARE YOU GOING TO FIX IT SO I CAN TALK TO ERIN VOSS?

WHAT IS THAT? WHERE'D YOU FIND IT?
AROUND. REMEMBER I GAVE YOUR HAND-MIRROR AWAY TO THE GIRL IN THE WELL? YOU CAN HAVE THIS ONE. IT'LL MAKE IT SO ERIN VOSS WILL WANT TO TALK TO YOU.

CLAC!
IF I CAN GET CLOSE ENOUGH TO HER, I DON'T ***NEED*** TO TALK TO HER. I CAN JUST USE THE HEAD KEY TO— WAIT A MINUTE. HOW IS THAT GOING TO HELP ME?

OH. EM.

GEE.

I WONDER IF PEOPLE SEE US DIFFERENTLY.
LIKE, LOOK. LOOK AT THAT WOMAN. IN THE COAT WITH THE FAKE FUR COLLAR.
WHY DOESN'T SHE COME SIT BACK HERE? THERE'S STILL AN EMPTY SEAT. RIGHT NEXT TO THAT KID. WHAT'S WRONG WITH THAT SEAT?
WHAT IF SHE'S JUST GETTING OFF AT THE NEXT STOP AND DOESN'T *WANT* TO SIT DOWN?
YEP. LOOK. SHE'S GETTING OFF. SEE?
MAYBE IT DOESN'T MATTER WHY SHE WOULDN'T SIT WITH US. MAYBE IT JUST SUCKS NOT KNOWING.
MOSTLY IT JUST SUCKS NOT KNOWING.

NOT EVEN FOUR IN THE AFTERNOON AND IT'S ALREADY HALFWAY DARK. NEW ENGLAND.
DO YOU THINK IT'S SAFE HERE? JAMAL SAID THIS IS A BAD PLACE.
LITTLE EAVESDROPPER. WE'LL TAKE A CAB BACK SO WE DON'T HAVE TO WAIT AROUND FOR THE BUS, HOW'S THAT? NOW, C'MON. LET'S GO SEE MISS VOSS AND GET THIS OVER WITH.
LET'S GET THIS SHIT UNDERWAY.
OKAY, BUT, *DUDE*. TRY NOT TO GET HER RILED UP. YOU KNOW HOW MUCH NOISE SHE MAKES WHEN SHE'S FREAKING OUT.
CALM THE FUCK DOWN. THIS WILL BE OVER IN TWO MINUTES. JUST MAKE SURE NO ONE BOTHERS US.
I DON'T WANT ANYONE COMING THROUGH THIS DOOR BEHIND ME.

THE WOLVES ARE IN THE KITCHEN! THERE'S THINGS THAT CAN HURT YOU IN THE KITCHEN! THERE'S KNIVES AND THERE'S FORKS AND THERE'S ALSO WOLVES! I DON'T GO IN THE KITCHEN!
"...PACK OF WOLVES HAD GOT INTO THE POTS OF LUCY'S MOTHER'S JAM..."
WHAT IF LUCY GETS EATEN? I SAID WE SHOULD WATCH TV. PICTURE BOOKS AREN'T SAFE. EVERYTHING IS BETTER ON TV!
NO, IT'S ALL RIGHT. NOTHING BAD HAPPENS. EXCEPT TO THE WOLVES. AND A JELLY SANDWICH.
HELP YOU, GIRL?
JUST LOOKING FOR THE LADIES. I SEE IT.
YOU'RE A NEW VOLUNTEER, AREN'T YOU? DO I KNOW YOU? SEEM LIKE WE BEEN ACQUAINTED ONCE BEFORE.
SORRY, DON'T THINK SO.
2A. I. GILLIAM
2B.
2C. E. VOSS
2D. D. ADAMS
2E. J. WILSON
2F.
2G. T. HOPPER
2H. G. LEE
2I. D. BROWN
2J. K. SMITH
2K.
2L. G. ENNIS
2M. A. LIFESON
2N. K. CHALLIS
2O. G. JONES
2P. N. PEART
2Q. V. CHONG
2R.
2S.
PERSONNEL ONLY
McCLELLAN HOSPITAL
2ND FLOOR

WHAT A WASTE OF RESOURCES YOU ARE, WOMAN. DO YOU DO ANYTHING BESIDES SLEEP AND EAT?
ACTUALLY—HEH. THAT'S LIKE 90% OF THE BLACK PEOPLE I KNOW, RIGHT THERE.

ALL RIGHT. TIME TO SMILE AND SAY "BOOBIES," YOU OUL' BITCH.

HELLO, ERIN.
MMMNNNN!

I WOULD'VE COME SOONER, BUT YOU KNOW HOW THE ANYWHERE KEY WORKS. I HAVE TO BE ABLE TO VISUALIZE WHERE I'M GOING.
OR *DO* YOU KNOW? THAT'S THE PROBLEM, ISN'T IT? I THOUGHT I CLEANED YOU OUT. YOU SHOULDN'T KNOW **ANYTHING**. BUT YOU SAW TYLER AND THOUGHT "RENDELL."
IF YOU REMEMBER ANYTHING, IT'S A PROBLEM. I CAN'T HAVE ANY RISKS TO MY IDENTITY. NOT WHEN I'M SO CLOSE TO OPENING THE BLACK DOOR AND BRINGING THEM THROUGH.
NO. NO. P-PLEASE. IT'S—IT'S— **WHITE.**

NNNNOOOO! WHITE! WHITE!
AH, CHRIST.
DUDE, I TOLT YOU, YOU GOTTA KEEP THINGS QUIET IN THERWARTHEFUCK?!
NO! DON'T!
AH! AH! PLEASE!
HOLD STILL. SHUT UP.

MISS VOSS?
WHITE. IT'S WHITE. DODGE.
MISS VOSS, THIS IS A TERRIBLE INVASION OF YOUR PRIVACY... IT'S JUST THE ONLY WAY. IF MY WHOLE FAMILY WASN'T IN DANGER, I WOULDN'T, I WOULDN'T EVER. BUT... IF YOU REALLY WERE MY DAD'S FRIEND, I KNOW YOU'D WANT TO HELP US.
DODGE. DODGE.
THANK YOU.

B-BUT... THERE'S NOTHING IN HERE. IT'S JUST... IT'S JUST...
...WHITE.
DOGE

RENDELL

NOTHING IN THERE, EXCEPT... WHO THE HELL IS THIS?
DODGE. DODGE.
DODGE... DODGE IS A PERSON? AND WHAT THE HELL IS HAPPENING TO HIM?
WAIT. I GET IT. YOU CAN'T REMEMBER THINGS. THOUGHTS GO WHITE AND FADE AWAY.
EXCEPT... DOES THAT MEAN THE STUFF IN YOUR HEAD ARE THINGS THAT JUST HAPPENED? DOES THAT MEAN—
OH, SHIT.
THIS IS A PRIVATE ROOM. WHAT ARE YOU DOING IN HERE, YOUNG LADY?

UHFF!
IF YOU'VE STOLEN ANYTHING—
—AAAAAAAAA AAHHH GOD! GOD HELP HELP GOD HELP!
"NO ONE PULLED OVER. I PROBABLY WAVED AT FIVE CABS AND NONE OF THEM STOPPED.
"WE MUST'VE RUN SIX BLOCKS BEFORE BODE THOUGHT OF THE MIRROR KEY."
TAXI

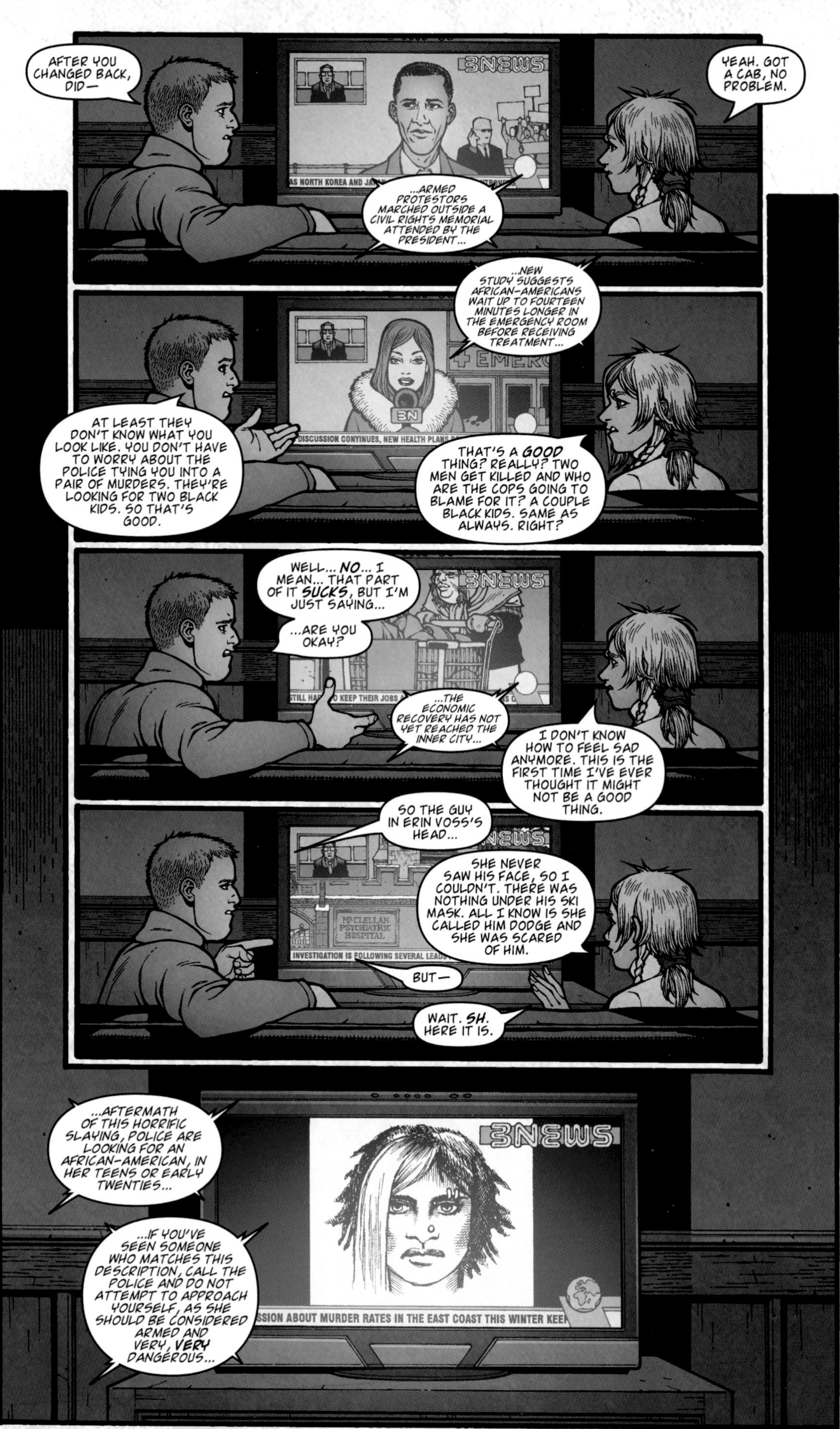
AFTER YOU CHANGED BACK, DID—
YEAH. GOT A CAB, NO PROBLEM.
3NEWS
AS NORTH KOREA AND JA
...ARMED PROTESTORS MARCHED OUTSIDE A CIVIL RIGHTS MEMORIAL ATTENDED BY THE PRESIDENT...
...NEW STUDY SUGGESTS AFRICAN-AMERICANS WAIT UP TO FOURTEEN MINUTES LONGER IN THE EMERGENCY ROOM BEFORE RECEIVING TREATMENT...
EMERG
BN
DISCUSSION CONTINUES, NEW HEALTH PLANS
AT LEAST THEY DON'T KNOW WHAT YOU LOOK LIKE. YOU DON'T HAVE TO WORRY ABOUT THE POLICE TYING YOU INTO A PAIR OF MURDERS. THEY'RE LOOKING FOR TWO BLACK KIDS. SO THAT'S GOOD.
THAT'S A GOOD THING? REALLY? TWO MEN GET KILLED AND WHO ARE THE COPS GOING TO BLAME FOR IT? A COUPLE BLACK KIDS. SAME AS ALWAYS. RIGHT?
WELL... NO... I MEAN... THAT PART OF IT SUCKS, BUT I'M JUST SAYING...
...ARE YOU OKAY?
3NEWS
...THE ECONOMIC RECOVERY HAS NOT YET REACHED THE INNER CITY...
I DON'T KNOW HOW TO FEEL SAD ANYMORE. THIS IS THE FIRST TIME I'VE EVER THOUGHT IT MIGHT NOT BE A GOOD THING.
SO THE GUY IN ERIN VOSS'S HEAD...
SHE NEVER SAW HIS FACE, SO I COULDN'T. THERE WAS NOTHING UNDER HIS SKI MASK. ALL I KNOW IS SHE CALLED HIM DODGE AND SHE WAS SCARED OF HIM.
McCLELLAN PSYCHIATRIC HOSPITAL
INVESTIGATION IS FOLLOWING SEVERAL LEADS
BUT—
WAIT. SH. HERE IT IS.
3NEWS
...AFTERMATH OF THIS HORRIFIC SLAYING, POLICE ARE LOOKING FOR AN AFRICAN-AMERICAN, IN HER TEENS OR EARLY TWENTIES...
...IF YOU'VE SEEN SOMEONE WHO MATCHES THIS DESCRIPTION, CALL THE POLICE AND DO NOT ATTEMPT TO APPROACH YOURSELF, AS SHE SHOULD BE CONSIDERED ARMED AND VERY, VERY DANGEROUS...
SSION ABOUT MURDER RATES IN THE EAST COAST THIS WINTER KEE

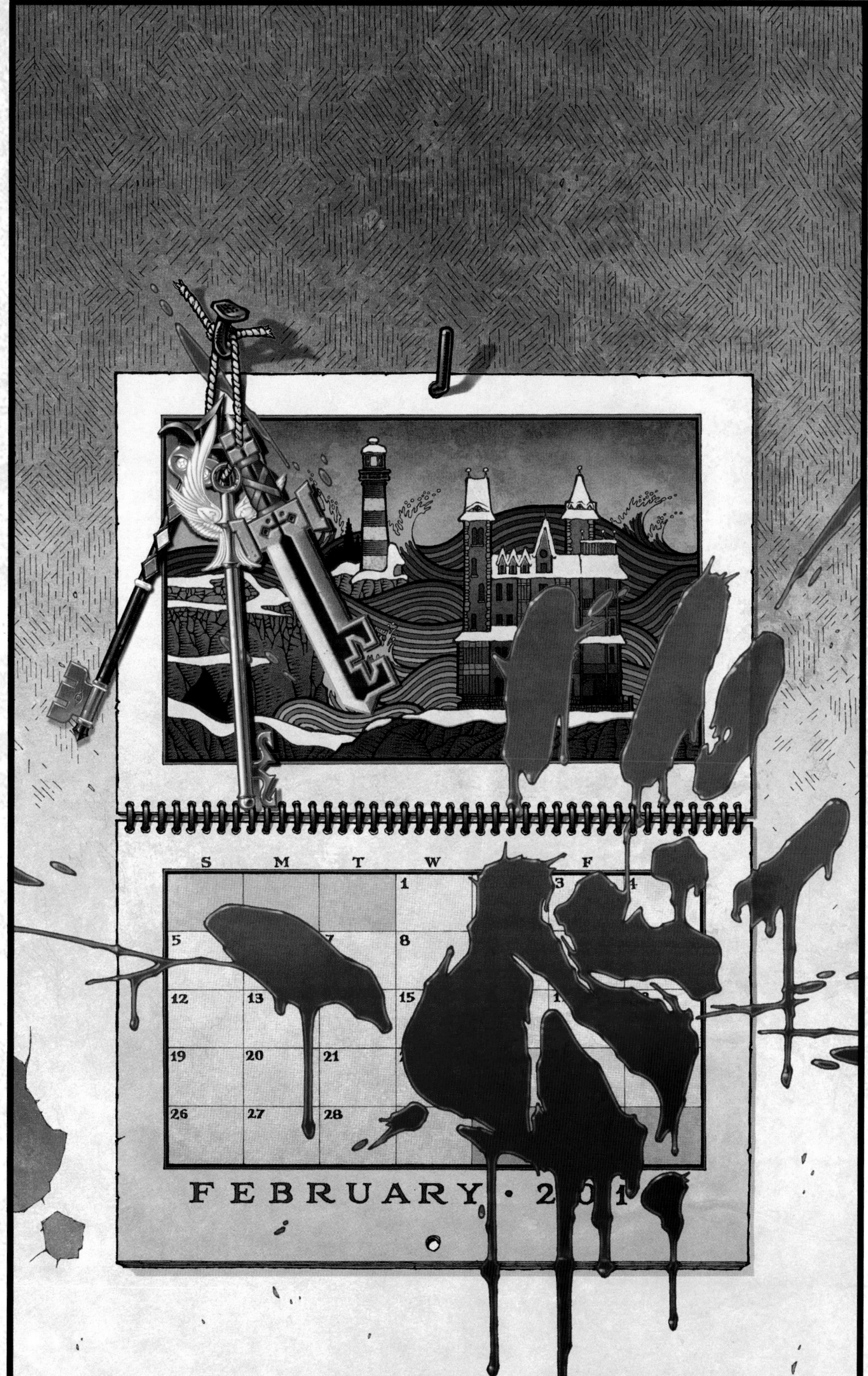
FEBRUARY

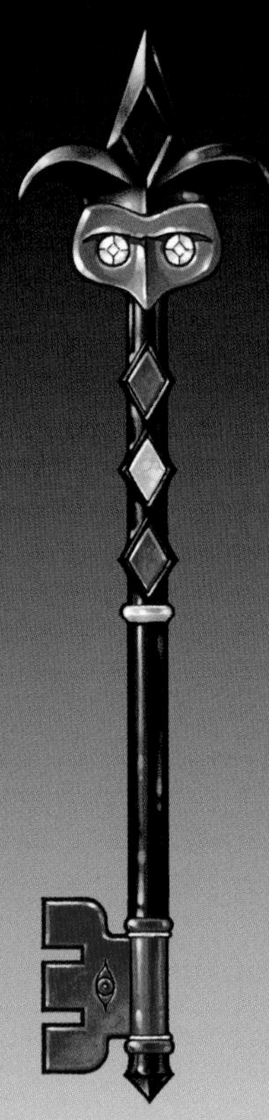

- KEYS TO THE KINGDOM -

Chapter Three

FEBRUARY

SCHLAMM!
GLUUUUAAAAP!
FEBRUARY
01
WED
EEEEE!
OH, MY GOD!
HOLY SHIT!
THEY'RE ANIMALS! WE'RE GETTING SLAUGHTERED OUT THERE!
LOCKE! GET IN THERE AND DO SOME DAMAGE BEFORE THEY PUT SOMEONE IN THE HOSPITAL!
M-MUH-ME? Y-YES, SIR!
DO SOME DAMAGE. DO SOME DAMAGE.
ALL RIGHT, B-BITCH! IT'S P-PAYBACK TIME!

FEBRUARY
02
THU
I JUST WISH SHE DIDN'T START CRYING WHEN SHE SAW ME. THAT'S THE PART I REALLY HATE.
YOUR MOTHER STARTED CRYING WHEN SHE SAW YOU? WHAT THE FUCK IS THAT?

SHE OVERREACTS TO EVERYTHING THESE DAYS.
IF IT CHEERS YOU UP, I THINK A COUPLE BRUISES MAKE A GUY LOOK DANGEROUS. IN A CUTE SORT OF WAY.
BESIDES. I SEE A BLACK EYE AND I JUST WANT TO KISS IT BETTER.

PAY ATTENTION TO WHAT JORDAN IS SAYING, DUDE. SHE LIKES MEN WHO ARE DAMAGED. THEY'RE EASIER PREY.
EAT MY ASS, BRINKER.
KEEP YOUR FANTASIES TO YOURSELF, BABE.
I WAS THINKING ABOUT A GOLD TOOTH FOR THE ONE I LOST. I DUNNO? STUPID OR BADASS?
BADASS. FOR SURE. YOU NEED A GOLD TOOTH AND YOU NEED TO GET RID OF THIS NASTY CAP WITH THAT FUCKING HILLBILLY HOOK—

MY CAP AND LURE? OH, NO, SORRY. I CAN'T. SEE, THE LURE WAS REALLY SPECIAL TO MY DAD AND I PROMISED I'D HOLD ONTO IT FOR A DAY WHEN I NEEDED SOME LUCK. AND THE HAT IS FROM THE DAY GIAMBI WENT 5 FOR 5 AND...
THIS IS RED SOX COUNTRY, DUDE, AND I HATE THAT FUCKING HAT AND THAT STUPID HOOK. TELL YOU WHAT. YOU THROW THEM AWAY, RIGHT NOW, BOTH OF THEM, AND WHEN WE GO TO THE BEACH TOMORROW NIGHT, I'LL—

FEBRUARY
03
FRI
I DON'T THINK YOU'RE DOING THAT RIGHT.
I KNOW I'M NOT DOING IT RIGHT. GODDAMN, I'M BAKED.

I WANT TO SIT BY THE FIRE. TY, YOU WANT TO GIMP OFF AND FIND ME ANOTHER HOT TODDY? YOU KNOW HOW I LIKE THEM, RIGHT?
SPOONFUL OF HONEY? SURE. GO GET WARM, I'LL MEET YOU—
—BRINKER, WHAT THE HELL ARE YOU DOING WITH THAT?

WHAT DO PEOPLE USUALLY DO WITH A FISHING ROD? I'M GOING FISHING. I'M GONNA CATCH SOMETHING I CAN STICK ON THE FIRE.
YOU'RE NOT GOING TO CATCH SOMETHING WITH THAT HOT DOG. MAYBE IF YOU HAD THE RIGHT FLY TO PLAY WITH.
YEAH, BRINKER, GO FIND A FLY TO PLAY WITH. LIKE YOUR OWN. ISN'T THAT WHAT YOU DO MOST NIGHTS?
BE CAREFUL WHAT YOU GOT ON YOUR LINE, TYLER. YOU GOT TO KNOW WHEN TO CUT BAIT.

LUCKY PRICK.
YOU THINK? SHE'S GOT A NICE LITTLE ASS ON HER, BUT IT SEEMS LIKE SHE MIGHT HAVE A FEW ISSUES.
HA! A FEW? YOU OUGHT TO MAJOR IN UNDERSTATEMENT WHEN YOU GET TO COLLEGE.

NAW, I'M NOT TALKING ABOUT HER. I'M TALKING HOCKEY. WE'VE GOT ANOTHER GAME AGAINST VOORHEES HIGH AT THE END OF THE MONTH.
I KNOW FOR A FACT HALF THOSE DUDES ARE ON THE JUICE. THE GUY WHO SELLS IT TO 'EM IS THE SAME FINE ENTREPRENEUR WHO SELLS ME WEED.
I DON'T KNOW IF YOU'VE NOTICED, BUT YOUR HOCKEY TEAM SUCKS. YOU EVER THINK YOU'VE BEEN BUYING THE WRONG ILLEGAL SUBSTANCES?

ARE YOU KIDDING? ANYONE WHO'D ARTIFICIALLY PUMP THEMSELVES UP TO WIN A MEANINGLESS HIGH SCHOOL HOCKEY GAME IS BEYOND PITIFUL. I'M GOING TO YALE, DUDE, AND I'M BRINGING A FULL-SIZE SET OF NUTS WITH ME.
ANYWAY. ALL TY HAS TO DO IS BABY HIS INJURY AND HE CAN SIT OUT THE GAME. THAT'S WHY HE'S A LUCKY PRICK. WHY SHOULDN'T HE TAKE A PASS? WE'VE LOST EVERY GAME SO FAR. NOTHING CAN SAVE THIS SEASON.
YEAH, BUT I THINK HE'LL PLAY ANYWAY. TYLER IS BIG ON TRYING TO FIX WHAT CAN'T BE FIXED. THAT'S WHY I LOVE THE GUY.

FEBRUARY
04
SAT
I DO, I LOVE TYLER. BUT I AGREE WITH YOU. IT WOULD BE SAFER IF SOMEONE ELSE KNEW WHAT HE DID WITH THIS—WHAT'D YOU CALL IT? OMEGA KEY? NOW IF SOMEONE ELSE KNOWS WHERE IT'S HIDDEN, THEN NO MATTER WHAT...
OH, CAN WE STOP TALKING ABOUT TYLER AND THE OMEGA KEY AND THE DARK LADY? I DIDN'T HAVE YOU OVER FOR A BUNCH OF TALK. I WANT TO DO SOMETHING FUN.
LIKE... FUN HOW? WHAT KIND OF FUN? I LIKE FUN.
ME TOO. AND IT'S TIME.

I WANT YOU TO OPEN UP TO ME. I WANT TO TAKE ONE OF YOUR HAPPIEST THOUGHTS AND PUT IT IN MY HEAD, AND I'LL TAKE ONE OF MY HAPPIEST THOUGHTS AND—
NO. THERE'S NO WAY.

WHY NOT? YOU CAN TRUST ME. YOU'VE SEEN ALL THE BAD STUFF IN MY HEAD. THERE CAN'T BE ANYTHING HALF SO BAD IN YOURS.
PLEASE. IT'LL FEEL GOOD. WHY CAN'T WE MAKE EACH OTHER FEEL GOOD?
FORGET IT. MY HEAD IS OFF-LIMITS.

YEAH. YOU'RE HAPPY TO GET YOUR HANDS UNDER MY SHIRT, BUT I'M NOT ALLOWED TO TOUCH YOUR OFF-LIMIT BITS.
I'VE NOTICED YOU DON'T WANT ME TO GET TOO CLOSE. TELL YOU WHAT, LET ME MAKE IT EASY FOR YOU TO PROTECT YOUR PRIVACY. GET OUT.
DAMMIT, I WISH I COULD STILL CRY.

FEBRUARY
05
SUN

FEBRUARY
06
MON
FINE! I'M FINE! I CAN'T EVEN FEEL 'EM. IT'S NO BIG DEAL. I JUST TRIPPED!
INTO WHAT? A BAG OF CATS?

MISHAP? MISHAP WITH WHAT? A CRATE FULL OF SCISSORS?
WILL YOU RELAX? YOU'RE CHANNELING MY MOTHER.
FEBRUARY
07
TUE

FEBRUARY
08
WED
OUT WITH IT, LUV. NO MORE PREVARICATIONS. WHAT HAPPENED TO YOU? YOU LOOK LIKE YOU LOST A CAGE MATCH WITH A PILE OF FORKS.
IT'S... COMPLICATED. AND... WEIRD. AND AFTER WHAT HAPPENED DOWN IN THE CAVE, I'M NOT GOING TO PULL YOU TWO INTO ANY MORE TROUBLE.
WHOA. YOU NEED TO STOP RIGHT THERE. YOU DON'T NEED TO PROTECT US FROM SHIT. FROM THE LOOKS OF YOU, YOU'RE THE ONE NEEDS PROTECTING.

IT'S NOT JUST ABOUT PROTECTING YOU. ALTHOUGH THERE IS THAT. BUT I ALSO DON'T WANT TO FRIGHTEN YOU GUYS OFF.
I JUST HAD THIS BIG, STUPID BREAK-UP WITH ZACK. I CAN'T LOSE ANYMORE FRIENDS RIGHT NOW.
YOU AND ZACK BROKE UP? OH, THAT'S... SO DREADFULLY...
...WONDERFUL.
DID YOU BREAK-UP BECAUSE HE COULDN'T HANDLE "WEIRD" AND "COMPLICATED"?
KIND OF. I PILED A LOT OF STRANGE SHIT ON HIM, AND HE WAS VERY COOL AND VERY ACCEPTING ABOUT IT.
BUT THEN I ASKED HIM TO TRUST ME ON SOMETHING AND IT WAS SCARY AND HE COULDN'T AND I WAS WRONG TO ASK.
SAME AS IT WOULD BE WRONG TO ASK YOU GUYS.
'EY, MATE, DID YOU JUST MAKE LITTLE QUOTATION SIGNS WITH YOUR FINGERS? THAT IS SO *CUTE*.
I GUESS I SHOULD TELL ZACK I'M SORRY, HUH?
NOT AT ALL. HE SHOULD APOLOGIZE TO YOU, FOR BEING AN INCORRIGIBLE PUSSY. FUCK HIM. WHATEVER HE WOULDN'T TRUST YOU ON—WHATEVER HE WAS AFRAID TO DO—I'D DO IT. TWICE.
A-*FUCKING*-MEN.
I... PROMISED JACKIE AFTER THE CAVE THAT I WOULDN'T PUT ANY OF YOU GUYS AT RISK AGAIN.
YEAH, WELL, *I* DIDN'T PROMISE ANYTHING.
ME, NEITHER. I HARDLY TAKE MY MARCHING ORDERS FROM MISS JACKIE VEDA AND I'M NOT AFRAID TO SAY SO TO HER—
HELLO, DEARS, WHAT'S UP THIS FINE DAY?
NOTHING!

LOVE ALL THE CLOSET SPACE IN THIS HOUSE.
KEYS TO THE KINGDOM

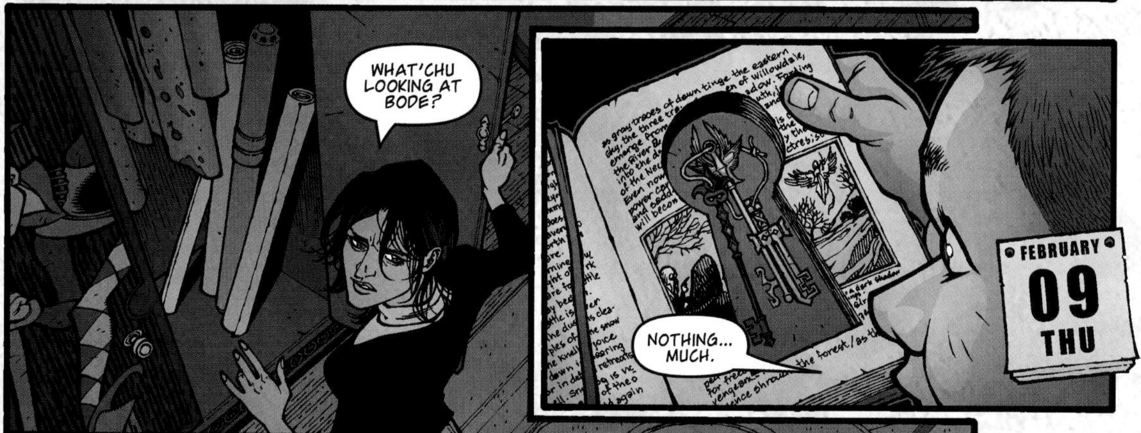
WHAT'CHU LOOKING AT BODE?
NOTHING... MUCH.
FEBRUARY
09
THU

OH, HELL. WHAT IS IT THIS TIME?
WHEN MOM OPENED IT THERE WAS NOTHING IN THERE. BUT SHE JUST USED ONE OF THE HOUSE KEYS FROM THE HARDWARE STORE.
BUT YOU USE THIS...
CLIC
...IT'S LIKE OPENING THE DOOR TO THE BATCAVE.

FEBRUARY
10
FRI

FEBRUARY
11
SAT

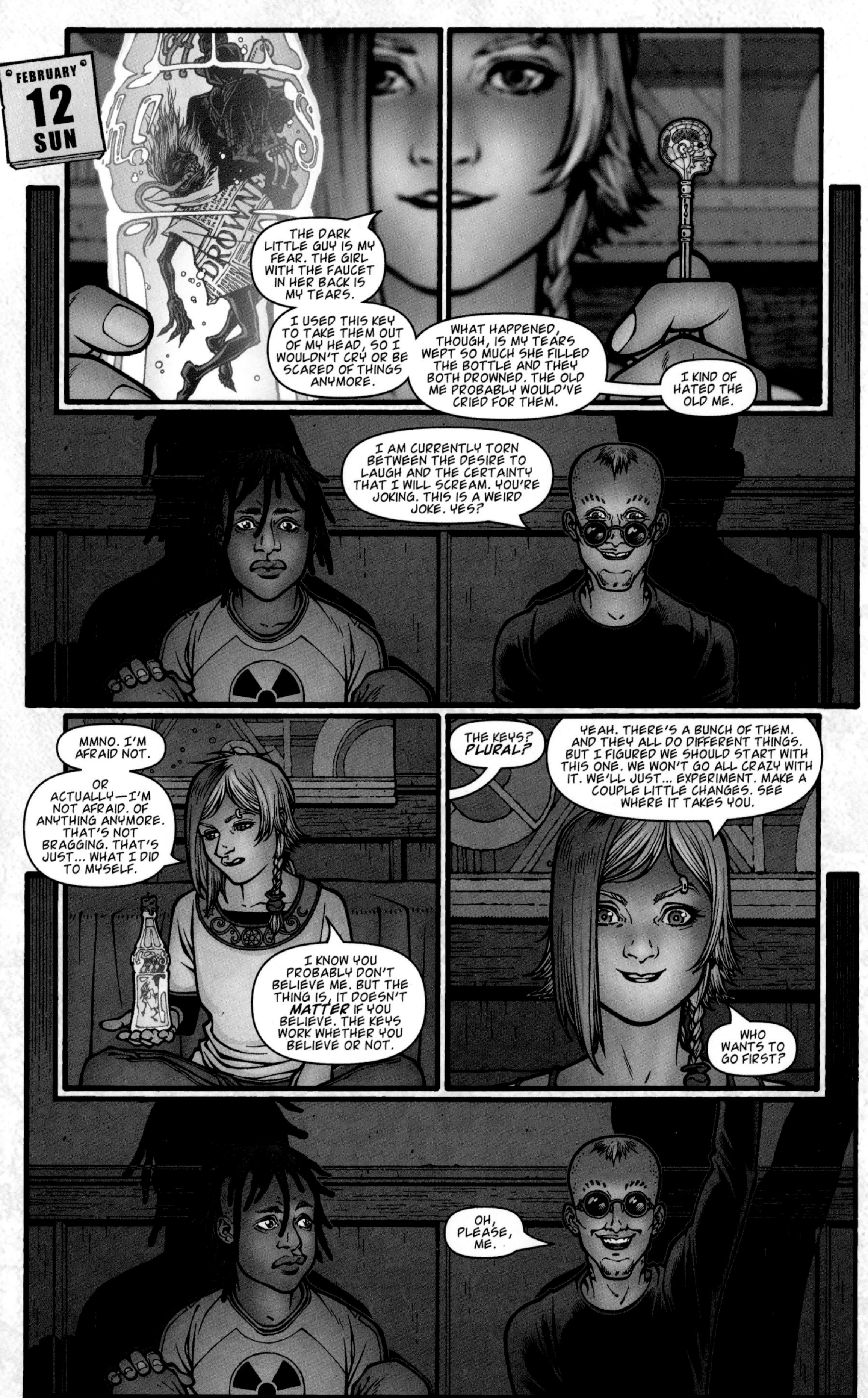
FEBRUARY 12 SUN
THE DARK LITTLE GUY IS MY FEAR. THE GIRL WITH THE FAUCET IN HER BACK IS MY TEARS.
I USED THIS KEY TO TAKE THEM OUT OF MY HEAD, SO I WOULDN'T CRY OR BE SCARED OF THINGS ANYMORE.
WHAT HAPPENED, THOUGH, IS MY TEARS WEPT SO MUCH SHE FILLED THE BOTTLE AND THEY BOTH DROWNED. THE OLD ME PROBABLY WOULD'VE CRIED FOR THEM.
I KIND OF HATED THE OLD ME.
I AM CURRENTLY TORN BETWEEN THE DESIRE TO LAUGH AND THE CERTAINTY THAT I WILL SCREAM. YOU'RE JOKING. THIS IS A WEIRD JOKE. YES?
MMNO. I'M AFRAID NOT.
OR ACTUALLY—I'M NOT AFRAID. OF ANYTHING ANYMORE. THAT'S NOT BRAGGING. THAT'S JUST... WHAT I DID TO MYSELF.
I KNOW YOU PROBABLY DON'T BELIEVE ME. BUT THE THING IS, IT DOESN'T MATTER IF YOU BELIEVE. THE KEYS WORK WHETHER YOU BELIEVE OR NOT.
THE KEYS? PLURAL?
YEAH. THERE'S A BUNCH OF THEM. AND THEY ALL DO DIFFERENT THINGS. BUT I FIGURED WE SHOULD START WITH THIS ONE. WE WON'T GO ALL CRAZY WITH IT. WE'LL JUST... EXPERIMENT. MAKE A COUPLE LITTLE CHANGES. SEE WHERE IT TAKES YOU.
WHO WANTS TO GO FIRST?
OH, PLEASE, ME.

KINSEY! IT'S SCOT! WE'VE GOT TO PUT IT BACK!
WE'VE GOT TO CAPTURE SCOT AND PUT HIS SANITY BACK BEFORE HE GETS HIMSELF EXPELLED! HE'S PERFORMING BYRON ON THE QUAD!
YEAH? SO?

FEBRUARY
13
MON

I CAN'T BELIEVE YOU'D JUST DRAG THEM INTO THIS WITHOUT TALKING TO ME! SOMETIMES I THINK YOU USED THE HEAD KEY TO TAKE OUT YOUR LAST FEW REMAINING I.Q. POINTS!
LOVE GETTING THIS LECTURE FROM A GUY WHO COULDN'T WAIT TO WHIP OUT HIS BIG MAGIC KEY TO IMPRESS SOME GIRL HE BARELY KNEW.
FEBRUARY
14
TUE
HAPPY VALENTINE'S DAY, TY. MAKE IT SPECIAL, WHY DON'T YOU? TAKE YOUR LEFT HAND FOR A ROMANTIC NIGHT OUT.

FEBRUARY
15
WED

BODE, WHAT ARE YOU *DOING?!*

PLAYING CARS.

I STEPPED ON YOUR GAZEBO. OOPSIE.

FEBRUARY
16
THU

SOMEONE COULD'VE COME BY AND SEEN YOU! SOMETIMES I THINK YOU AND KINSEY ARE MORE DANGEROUS THAN THE DARK LADY!

ALL YOU DO IS YELL. YOU'RE TURNING INTO MOM. YOU'VE EVEN GOT THE CRUTCH.

FEBRUARY
17
FRI
KINSEY! BODE!
C'MON, GUUUUUUUYS! I SAID I WAS SORRY! THIS IS SERIOUS DOWN HERE!

FEBRUARY
18
SAT
GET A KNIFE, GET A KNIFE, IT'S TIME TO HAVE FUN...
TAKE THE KNIFE, TAKE THE KNIFE, STICK IT INTO SOMEONE...

FEBRUARY
19
SUN
...SAYS HE'S STILL RECOVERING, BUT THERE'S NO WAY TO MEASURE THE POSSIBLE BRAIN DAMAGE UNTIL HE WAKES UP...
YEAH, A DAY OR A YEAR... IF...
NO, JUST TIRED...
BIG HUG TO EACH OF YOU... I'LL BE VISITING AGAIN SOON, PROMISE.

FEBRUARY
20
MON
PROFESSOR CORNWELL IS A FUCKING BITCHASS DYKE!
SHE GAVE ME HOUSE DETENTION FOR A WEEK. I CAN'T EVEN EAT IN THE CAFETERIA! I HAVE TO STAY IN THE SHITTY FACULTY HOUSING AND EAT DINNERS IN MY ROOM AND STUDY TO RETAKE THE TEST NEXT FRIDAY.
IT'S NOT MY FAULT I WAS LATE TO THE TEST! MY ALARM DIDN'T GO OFF!
WELL, YEAH, BUT... I MEAN... THE CLASS IS AT TWO IN THE AFTERNOON, JORDAN.
COL. ADAM CRAIS
MAY 18 1736
"The Dreams o
of Free Men
Army of Shado
as impossib
strike d
I SLEEP LATE! I'M ALMOST 19, IT GOES WITH THE TERRITORY!
SHE GOT ALL WEEPY WHEN SHE CALLED ME INTO THE OFFICE, LIKE SHE'S THE ONE BEING PUNISHED. I OUGHTA SET FIRE TO HER ETHICAL LITTLE PRIUS. THAT'D GIVE HER SOMETHING TO CRY ABOUT.
I'VE GOT AN ALTERNATIVE IDEA. INSTEAD OF TORCHING HER CAR AND GETTING KICKED OUT, HOW ABOUT YOU AND ME CAMP OUT IN THE LIBRARY AND I HELP YOU STUDY AND YOU PASS WITH AN "A" INSTEAD?
TY. WHY THE FUCK ARE YOU SO NICE TO ME, ANYWAY?
I DIDN'T OVERSLEEP THE CLASS. I JUST DIDN'T STUDY AND I KNEW I'D FAIL, SO I SKIPPED. I'M THE BITCH, TYLER, NOT MRS. CORNWELL.
YOU AREN'T THE ONLY PERSON TO EVER DO SOME THINGS THEY WISH THEY COULD TAKE BACK.
I WISH YOU WERE HUNG UP ON SOME OTHER GIRL. SOME BETTER GIRL.
HEY. HEY. YOU MAKE ME LAUGH. YOU MAKE ME CRAZY. YOU'RE THE COOLEST PERSON I KNOW. TRUTH IS, SOMETIMES I FEEL LIKE I'M HALF IN LO—
NO! STOP! SH.
DON'T BE STUPID. DON'T SAY SOMETHING STUPID. YOU DON'T KNOW ANYTHING ABOUT ME EXCEPT I'M PRETTY AND MAKE OUT REAL NICE WHEN I'M DRUNK.
IF YOU KNEW ME—IF YOU REALLY KNEW SOME OF THE LOUSY THINGS I'M CAPABLE OF—YOU'D NEVER FORGIVE ME.
YEAH, WELL, I THINK THE SAME THING ABOUT MYSELF SOMETIMES. MAYBE BEST WE CAN DO IS BE WILLING TO FORGIVE EACH OTHER.
I'M GOING TO RUN HOME AND GET MY BOOKS AND NOTES. WE'RE GOING TO KICK THIS TEST IN THE ASS.
YEAH. OH-OKAY. SURE. THANK YOU, TYLER.

THE BEST THING ABOUT NOT HAVING ANY GRIEF IS THAT IT'S TOTALLY EASY TO IGNORE HIM WHEN I SEE HIM IN THE HALL. BEFORE I TOOK OUT MY TEARS, I WOULD'VE SPENT THE WHOLE MONTH CRYING MY EYES OUT.
FEBRUARY 21 TUE
YOU EVER THINK THE REASON ZACK DIDN'T WANT TO OPEN UP TO YOU AND SHARE ONE OF HIS HAPPIEST THOUGHTS IS BECAUSE HE DOESN'T HAVE ANY TO SHARE?
OF COURSE, YOU ALREADY KNOW MY SADLY EMPTY HEAD IS YOURS TO PLUNDER.
SPEAKING FOR MYSELF, I'D SELL A KIDNEY TO HAVE YOUR HAPPIEST THOUGHT IN MY HEAD FOR A DAY.
YOU DON'T NEED TO DO THAT.
SNAP OUT OF IT, KAVANAUGH! I SAID I'D HELP YOU WITH YOUR PRESENTATION, I DIDN'T SAY I'D WRITE IT FOR YOU! YOU'VE BEEN WEIRD ALL NIGHT. WHAT THE HELL IS GOING ON IN YOUR HEAD?
YOU EVER HAVE A MEMORY THAT ISN'T YOURS? A PERFECT MEMORY OF SOMEONE ELSE'S FATHER, AND SOMEONE ELSE'S STARS?
AUW. AUW, DAMMIT. ARE YOU HIGH ON SOMETHING? WHAT DID YOU TAKE? WHO GAVE IT TO YOU?
FEBRUARY 22 WED
NOW, NOW. DON'T OVERREACT. KINSEY SHARED A LITTLE SOMETHING OF HERS, BUT IT ISN'T... ISN'T HARMFUL. SHE SHARED HER PRIVATE STARS WITH ME. JUST WITH ME.
UNH. SORRY. DOZED OFF. WHERE'D WE—
SH. YOU'RE WORKING HARDER ON THIS THAN I AM. GO AHEAD AND REST, TYLER. REST A LITTLE.

KINSEY, GIRL. I'VE DECIDED I HAVE ANOTHER MEMORY I WANT TO SHARE WITH—
JAMAL? SAY WHAT... WHAT ARE YOU TWO...
OH, HEY, DUDE. I WAS JUST—WE BEEN TRADING MEMORIES OF OUR DADS ALL AFTERNOON. IT'S AWESOME. SO AWESOME.

KINSEY? YOU AND HIM ARE—I THOUGHT THAT WAS... WAS OUR THING.
SCOT. WE'RE JUST FOOLING AROUND A LITTLE. IT'S NOT—IT'S NO BIG DEAL.

AND I THOUGHT WE WERE MATES, MATE.
NO, YOU THOUGHT I WAS YOUR FUNNY ETHNIC SIDEKICK. OR YOUR CHEERLEADER. OR SOMETHING. FAR AS I'M CONCERNED, YOU DISQUALIFIED YOUR CLAIM TO KINSEY WHEN YOU WERE WILLING TO LET HER DROWN TO SAVE YOUR OWN ASS, AND ME WITH HER.
GUYS... JAMAL, THAT'S NOT FAIR... SCOT... NEITHER OF YOU HAVE A CLAIM...

FEBRUARY
23
THU

TAK
TAK
TAK
TAK
TAK
JORDAN. SST. JORDAN!
TY! WHAT ARE YOU DOING HERE?
YOU GOT A B! THAT'S AWESOME! I TOLD YOU WE'D HAVE SOMETHING TO CELEBRATE. I GOT SOME WINE FROM MY MOM'S CELLAR—FAMILY LABEL STUFF—AND SNUCK OUT AND—
HEY, GATES? THE FUCK?
AH, SHIT. LOCKE. WHAT'S GOING ON?
DUDE, I AM SO SORRY ABOUT THIS. FOR THE RECORD, THIS NEVER WOULD'VE HAPPENED IF I WASN'T TOTALLY WRECKED.
JORDAN AND ME DON'T EVEN LIKE EACH OTHER. YOU KNOW THAT.
CLIC
IF YOU KNEW HE MIGHT COME BY, WHY'D YOU TELL ME TO COME OVER? WHY'D YOU GET ME STONED? EVEN BY YOUR STANDARDS, JORDAN, THIS IS A NEW LOW. LOCKE ISN'T A BAD GUY.
MAYBE THAT'S WHY I DID IT.
UH. IS THAT SUPPOSED TO MAKE SENSE?
NOT TO YOU.
FEBRUARY
24
FRI

HEY. *HEY.* WHERE DOES THE TRASH GO?
MM? THE DUMPSTERS BEHIND THE CAFETERIA.
DO YOU KNOW HOW OFTEN THEY'RE EMPTIED?
I DON'T KNOW. LET ME THINK. I GUESS—PRO'LY THE LAST SATURDAY OF EVERY MONTH. Y'KNOW. TODAY.
WAIT! *WAIT!*
C'MON. C'MON, PLEASE...
FEBRUARY
25
SAT

FEBRUARY
26
SUN
A'S

FEBRUARY
27
MON
A'S

FEBRUARY
28
TUE
HOW THEY BITING?

GOOD. JUST PULLED IN A MACKEREL. SIX POUNDS, AT LEAST.
MUST BE NICE. NOT BEING ABLE TO CRY. I GOT TO GIVE THAT A WHIRL.
NO, YOU DON'T. I WISH I HADN'T DONE IT. MAYBE IF I COULD STILL REMEMBER WHAT IT'S LIKE TO FEEL SAD, I WOULDN'T HAVE GONE AND FUCKED THINGS UP WITH MY BEST FRIENDS.
JAMAL AND SCOT WON'T TALK TO EACH OTHER ANY MORE AND JACKIE TOLD ME SHE CAN'T BE FRIENDS WITH SOMEONE SO... RECKLESS WITH OTHER PEOPLE'S TRUST. AND SHE'S RIGHT. WHAT A MESS I MADE, TYLER.

HEY. I THOUGHT YOU WERE OPPOSED TO USING THE KEYS EXCEPT WHEN WE'RE UNDER ATTACK. WHY ARE YOU WEARING THAT?

BECAUSE I'M SICK OF FEELING WEAK.

OH, TY. I DON'T KNOW. THAT THING MAKES YOU—WHAT—THREE TIMES AS STRONG AS YOU USUALLY ARE?

YEAH.

THAT'S PRETTY MUCH WHAT I WAS THINKING.

IT'S NOT THE KIND OF THING YOU JUST WANT TO WALK AROUND IN. SOMEONE COULD GET HURT.

Smash!
ICON
LOCKE
16
FEBRUAR
29

- KEYS TO THE KINGDOM -

Chapter Four

CASUALTIES

TWO-FISTED TALES OF THE UNCANNY!!
SQUADRON STRANGE!
©IDW
¢49
22
• JAN •
2011
WHEN SQUADRON STRANGE ACCEPT A MISSION FROM A GHOST, THEY FIND THEMSELVES ON THEIR MOST PERILOUS RAID EVER — STRAIGHT INTO A HAUNTED MANSION!
THIS DOES NOT COMPUTE. IT IS OUR DIRECTIVE TO STAY ALIVE... HOW WE CAN HOPE TO ACHIEVE THAT GOAL BY TAKING ORDERS FROM THE DEAD?
WE HAVE A BETTER CHANCE OF SURVIVAL BY SURRENDERING OURSELVES TO THE ENEMY!
CAN IT, TRASHCAN HEAD! THE THING WE'RE FIGHTIN' AIN'T TAKING PRISIONERS...
IF HE DOESN'T KILL YOU TRYING TO GIVE YOUR COWARDLY CIRCUITS UP...
THEN I WILL!
I DON'T SEE HOW WE HAVE ANY CHOICE.
WE'RE GONNA HAVE TO TRUST THIS SHADY SPIRIT...
IF WE DON'T WANNA WIND UP JUST LIKE HIM!
SQUADRON STRANGE! AND LOCKE & KEY created by J.H. + G.R.
—JOE HILL & GABRIEL RODRÍGUEZ—
Shell-shocked Storytellers of...
"CASUALTIES"
Concussed Colorist: JAY FOTOS
Lacerated Letterer: ROBBIE ROBBINS
Ennui-Engulfed Editor: CHRIS RYALL
KEEP YOUR HANKIES HANDY, TRUE BELIEVERS... BECAUSE IN THIS ISSUE...
SOMEONE DIES

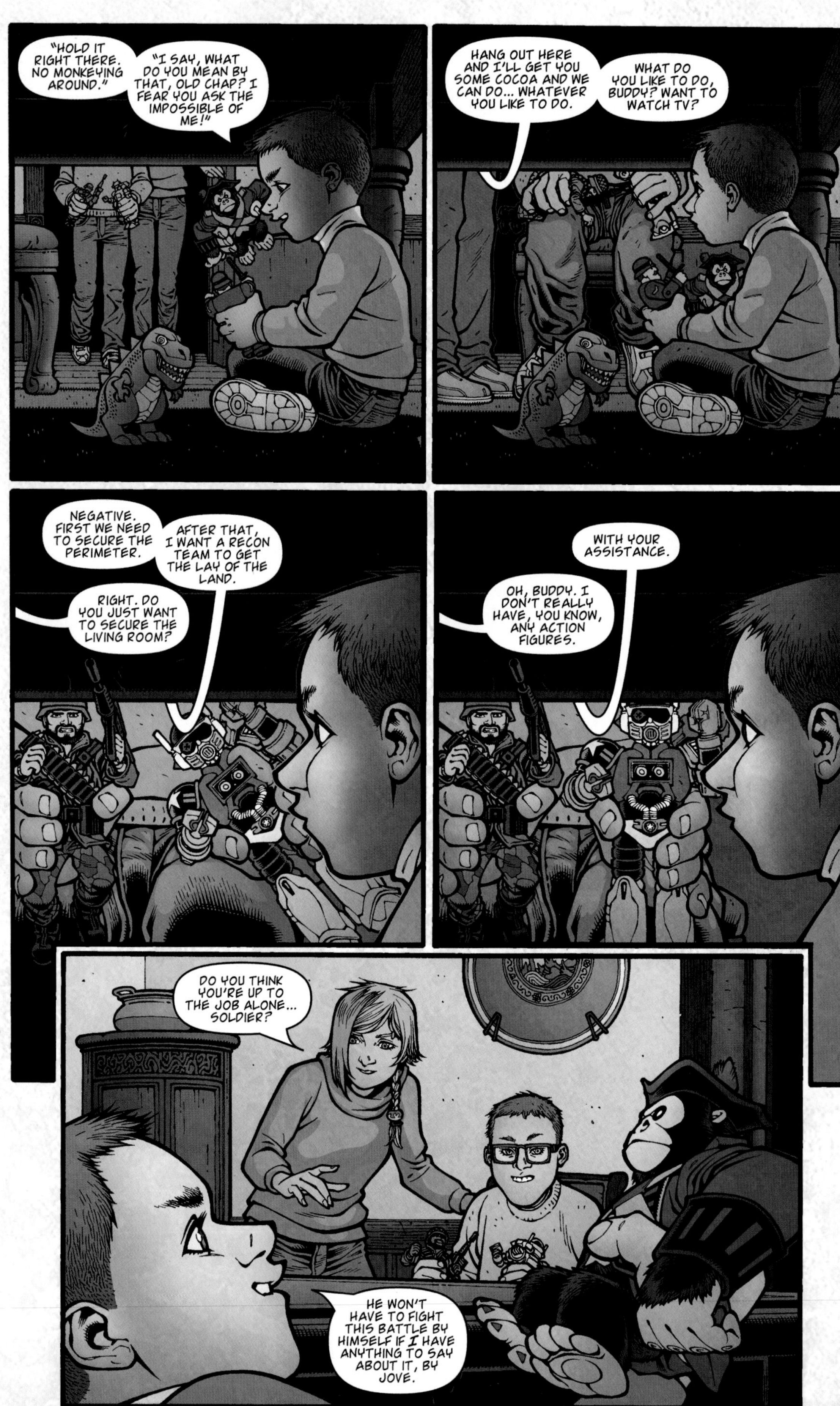
"HOLD IT RIGHT THERE. NO MONKEYING AROUND."
"I SAY, WHAT DO YOU MEAN BY THAT, OLD CHAP? I FEAR YOU ASK THE IMPOSSIBLE OF ME!"
HANG OUT HERE AND I'LL GET YOU SOME COCOA AND WE CAN DO... WHATEVER YOU LIKE TO DO.
WHAT DO YOU LIKE TO DO, BUDDY? WANT TO WATCH TV?
NEGATIVE. FIRST WE NEED TO SECURE THE PERIMETER.
AFTER THAT, I WANT A RECON TEAM TO GET THE LAY OF THE LAND.
RIGHT. DO YOU JUST WANT TO SECURE THE LIVING ROOM?
WITH YOUR ASSISTANCE.
OH, BUDDY. I DON'T REALLY HAVE, YOU KNOW, ANY ACTION FIGURES.
DO YOU THINK YOU'RE UP TO THE JOB ALONE... SOLDIER?
HE WON'T HAVE TO FIGHT THIS BATTLE BY HIMSELF IF *I* HAVE ANYTHING TO SAY ABOUT IT, BY JOVE.

THAT'S A REALLY CUTE BRITISH ACCENT, BODE. YOU BEEN PRACTICING?
UH-HUH. WITH SCOT. AND ZACK IS GOING TO TEACH ME FENCING SO I CAN SWORDFIGHT WITH A BRITISH ACCENT.
HEY, KINSEY, HOW COME THEY HAVEN'T BEEN OVER LATELY? LIKE SCOT OR ZACK OR JAMAL... OR... OR JACKIE... OR ANYONE?

BECAUSE I WASN'T A VERY GOOD FRIEND, BODE.
KINSEY? ARE YOU OKAY?
YOU KNOW ME, KID. NOTHING MUCH GETS ME DOWN ANYMORE. YOU THINK YOU CAN HELP ME WITH SOMETHING?

I PROMISED COACH WHEDON I'D WATCH RUFUS THIS AFTERNOON. SHE'S BUSY WITH ASSESSMENTS. ZACK CAN'T WATCH HIM BECAUSE IT'S SUNDAY AND HE GOES TO BOSTON ON THE WEEKEND FOR HIS RESEARCH PAPER.
JACKIE WATCHES HIM SOMETIMES, BUT SHE'S OFF LOOKING AT YALE THIS WEEKEND. SO IT'S JUST ME. CAN YOU GO ON MISSIONS WITH RUFUS? I THINK HE'D LIKE THAT.
QUITE, QUITE.

I'LL BE BACK WITH COCOA. YOU TWO MAKE FRIENDS.
THAT OUGHT TO BE EASY. ALL WE NEED IS A BUNCHA BANANAS FOR MONKEYFACE HERE.

I'VE HAD TO WORK WITH SOME SORRY RECRUITS BEFORE BUT GETTING A GORILLA ASSIGNED TO SQUADRON STRANGE IS THE LAST STRAW!
NOW, NOW, OLD CHAP. *I* DON'T MUCH LIKE GOING TO WAR BESIDE AN ARMED VACUUM CLEANER, BUT WE DON'T GET TO PICK WHO WE FIGHT WITH... OR THE THINGS WE FIGHT ***AGAINST***.
THE COSTUMED APE MAKES A LOGICAL POINT. WE SHOULD FIND A SECURE POSITION AND PREPARE TO DEFEND OURSELVES.

GOOD IDEA. LET'S REGROUP AT HEADQUARTERS.
SOUNDS LIKE A PLAN.
AS LONG AS HEADQUARTERS ISN'T DARK. I'M A LITTLE SCARED OF THE DARK.

SOMEWHERE IN FRANCE, 1941... SQUADRON STRANGE FINDS THEMSELVES CUT OFF AND SURROUNDED. IN OTHER WORDS...
...THEY'VE GOT THE ENEMY RIGHT WHERE THEY WANT THEM!
OUTFLANKED... OUTNUMBERED... IT SEEMS HOPELESS! BUT IT'S ALWAYS DARKEST BEFORE THE LIGHT! I'LL HAVE TO PLAY MY BEST TO KEEP THE MORALE OF MY COMRADES UP!
WATCH OUT, JACK NIFE! THESE DANGEROUS DINOS ARE LOOKING TO TAKE A BITE OUT OF US!
YEAH, WELL, I HOPE THEY LIKE THE TASTE OF MY KNUCKLES... CAUSE I'LL BE SERVING THEM UP ALL NIGHT!
GAKGAKGAKGAKGAKGAKGAK
TIME TO GET PREHISTORIC ON THESE STINKIN'...

OH, HELLO. WERE WE BEING TOO LOUD?

YOU AREN'T BOTHERING ME.
YOU CAN SEE ME?
YES, SIR.

KNOCK KNOCK!
WHO'S THERE?
MY OLD PAL SMITH AND HIS BUDDY, MR. WESTON! BLAM! BLAMABLAM BLAMBLAM!
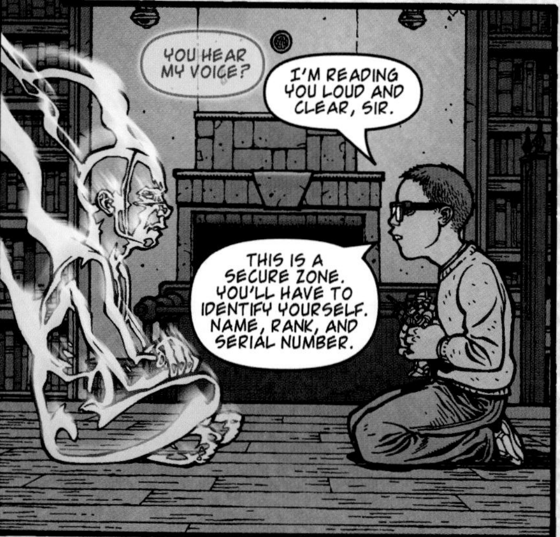
YOU HEAR MY VOICE?
I'M READING YOU LOUD AND CLEAR, SIR.
THIS IS A SECURE ZONE. YOU'LL HAVE TO IDENTIFY YOURSELF. NAME, RANK, AND SERIAL NUMBER.

NAME, RANK, AND... SERGEANT SAMUEL LESSER, U.S. ARMY. SERIAL NUMBER... 867-5309. CURRENTLY DECEASED. DO YOU KNOW WHAT DECEASED MEANS?
SIR, YES SIR.

IT MEANS DEAD.
DOES THAT SCARE YOU?
NO SIR. THAT'S WHAT HAPPENS IN WAR. PEOPLE DIE. THE REST OF US HAVE TO CARRY ON.
THAT'S RIGHT, SOLDIER.
SIR, IF YOU DON'T MIND MY ASKING, DID YOU GET IT IN BATTLE?
I DID. THE ENEMY LED ME INTO A TRAP AND CUT ME DOWN. RIGHT HERE IN THIS HALLWAY.
THIS MAY LOOK LIKE AN OLD HOUSE, BUT YOU AND BODE HAVE IT EXACTLY RIGHT. IT'S A BATTLEFIELD. THE FIGHTING HAS CLAIMED MANY LIVES.
I'M HARDLY THE ONLY CASUALTY IN THIS WAR.
I'M SORRY, SIR. I'LL PLAY TAPS FOR YOU, IF YOU WANT.
I CAN PLAY THE FRENCH HORN VERY WELL.
I'M SURE YOU CAN.
CAN I DO ANYTHING ELSE FOR YOU, SIR? TO HONOR YOUR SACRIFICE?
YOU CAN TALK TO ME. I HAVEN'T TALKED WITH ANYONE IN A WHILE. EVEN IN LIFE I... I DIDN'T SOCIALIZE MUCH WITH THE ENLISTED MEN.
LONE WOLF, SIR? THEY MAKE THE BEST SOLDIERS.

IF YOU DON'T MIND CHEWING THE FAT WITH A LOWLY PRIVATE, I'LL FALL IN WITH YOU.
NOT HERE, THOUGH. OTHER PEOPLE CAN'T SEE ME. THEY MIGHT WONDER WHO YOU'RE TALKING TO.

I DON'T KNOW IF ANYONE WILL CARE, SIR. EVERYONE ALREADY THINKS I'M SECTION-8.
BESIDES, I PROMISED KINSEY I'D STAY IN THE PARLOR. SHE'S THE REGIONAL COMMANDER HERE.
YOU CAN DISREGARD HER ORDERS, PRIVATE. I OUTRANK HER.

YOU SEE MY STRIPES DON'T YOU?
SIR, YES SIR. JUST... WE'RE HAVING COCOA AND BLUEBERRY COBBLER AT 1900 HOURS.

I'LL GET YOU BACK BY THEN.
WELL... ALL RIGHT.

MY WORD, I BELIEVE THESE BRONTOSAURI CAN BE TRAINED!

AFTER YOU'RE DONE, I WANT YOU TO TAKE THE KEY TO THE WINE CELLAR. JUST PUT IT SOMEPLACE I WON'T FIND IT. CAN YOU DO THAT?
SHOULDN'T BE A PROBLEM.
YOUR NAME IS RUFUS. YOU'RE THE TRACK COACH'S SON. YOU LIVE WITH THE ONE CALLED ZACK WELLS.
THAT'S AFFIRMATIVE, SIR. WHAT ABOUT YOUR FAMILY? DO THEY KNOW WHAT HAPPENED TO YOU?

I'D BE GLAD TO WRITE SOME LETTERS TO YOUR MOTHER IF YOU WANT. I KNOW IF I FELL IN BATTLE, I'D WANT SOMEONE TO LET MY MOM KNOW I LOVED HER.
THANK YOU, RUFUS. THAT'S VERY KIND. YOU DON'T HAVE TO DO THAT.

IT'D BE MY HONOR, SIR. I WRITE VERY GOOD LETTERS. I KNOW ALL THE LETTERS OF THE ALPHABET UP TO W AND I CAN WRITE THEM UPPER-CASE AND LOWER-CASE.
A, B, C, D, L, F, R, W...
THAT'S VERY GOOD, RUFUS. BUT YOU DON'T NEED TO WRITE MY MOTHER FOR ME.

TELL ME ABOUT *YOUR* MOTHER. IS SHE A GOOD MOTHER? DOES SHE LOVE YOU?
OF COURSE SHE DOES. SHE LOVES ME BIG AS THE MOON. SHE ALWAYS SAYS SO.

MY MOTHER WAS SORRY SHE HAD ME.
I'M SURE THAT ISN'T TRUE, SIR.
IT IS. I WAS AN ACCIDENT. SHE OFTEN SAID SO. MY FATHER HATED ME FOR BEING SMARTER THAN HIM.

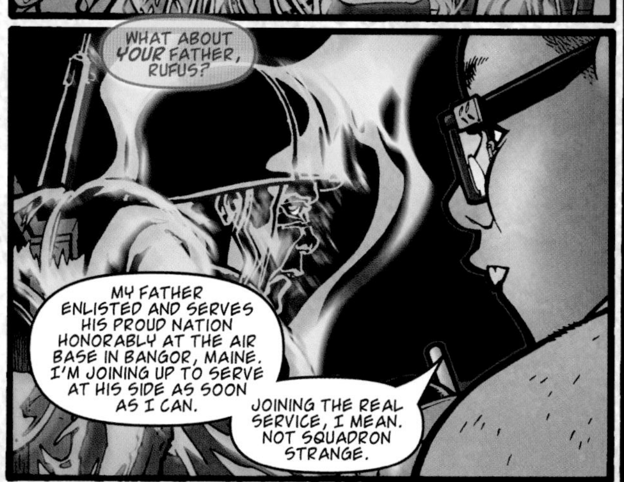
WHAT ABOUT *YOUR* FATHER, RUFUS?
MY FATHER ENLISTED AND SERVES HIS PROUD NATION HONORABLY AT THE AIR BASE IN BANGOR, MAINE. I'M JOINING UP TO SERVE AT HIS SIDE AS SOON AS I CAN.
JOINING THE REAL SERVICE, I MEAN. NOT SQUADRON STRANGE.

SIR, I'M SURE BOTH OF YOUR PARENTS MISS YOU.
I'M SURE THEY DON'T. THEY'RE DEAD, TOO. KILLED. IN A WAY, THEY WERE ALSO CASUALTIES IN THIS WAR.

SOMETIMES I FIGHT VELOCIRAPTOR MEN AND SOMETIMES I FIGHT SADDAM HUSSEIN, BUT THEY'RE JUST PRETEND.

THE ENEMY I'M TALKING ABOUT LIVES IN THE SAME HOUSE WITH YOU. HE'S NOT WHAT HE APPEARS TO BE. HE LOOKS LIKE A BOY, BUT HE'S NOT.

HE'S BOTH MORE THAN THAT, AND QUITE A BIT LESS. AND...

...HE'S ***WATCHING YOU RIGHT NOW!***

DON'T BE AFRAID. HE SEES YOU, BUT HE CAN'T SEE ***ME***, AND HE CAN'T HEAR EITHER OF US. HE DOESN'T KNOW WE'RE TALKING.

IF HE THINKS ANYTHING, HE THINKS YOU'RE TALKING TO YOUR TOYS.

WHY IS HE WATCHING ME? HOW CAN HE DO THAT?

DON'T BE AFRAID. HE'S SEARCHING FOR SOMETHING. HE'S BEEN LOOKING OVER THE HOUSE ALL NIGHT, AND AT THE MOMENT HE'S LOOKING AT YOU.

HE MAY ALSO BE KEEPING AN EYE ON YOU BECAUSE HE KNOWS YOU'RE DANGEROUS TO HIM.
I TOLD YOU THIS HOUSE IS A BATTLEGROUND BUT I DIDN'T SAY WHAT'S BEING FOUGHT FOR HERE. MAYBE I SHOULD SHOW YOU.
FALL IN, SOLDIER.
OOO, I... I DON'T LIKE THE DARK. REQUEST PERMISSION TO ABORT MISSION.
NEGATIVE, SOLDIER...

...I BROUGHT A LIGHT.

WHAT IS THIS PLACE?
THE CHAMBER OF THE LIVING SHADOWS.
IS IT... IS IT SAFE?

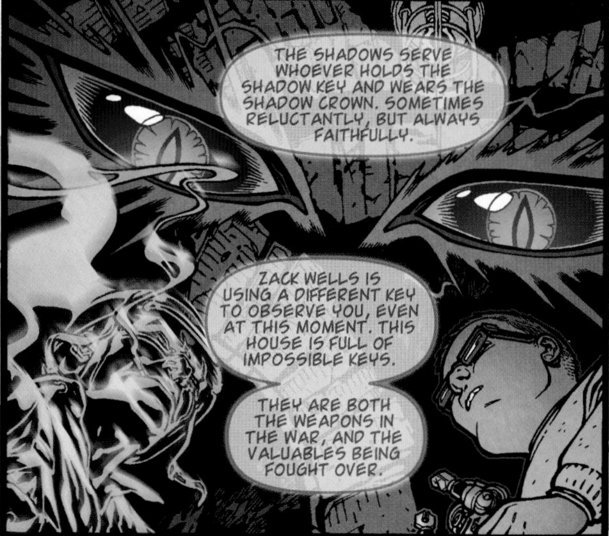

THE SHADOWS SERVE WHOEVER HOLDS THE SHADOW KEY AND WEARS THE SHADOW CROWN. SOMETIMES RELUCTANTLY, BUT ALWAYS FAITHFULLY.
ZACK WELLS IS USING A DIFFERENT KEY TO OBSERVE YOU, EVEN AT THIS MOMENT. THIS HOUSE IS FULL OF IMPOSSIBLE KEYS.
THEY ARE BOTH THE WEAPONS IN THE WAR, AND THE VALUABLES BEING FOUGHT OVER.

I'M SCARED. I DON'T LIKE IT HERE. I THINK I SHOULD GO. I THINK I WANT TO GO HOME.
HOME IS BETTER? WITH HIM LIVING THERE?
YOUR MOTHER MUST KNOW THE TRUTH ABOUT HIM. SHE MUST KNOW HOW DANGEROUS HE IS. AND YET SHE SHELTERS HIM. GIVES AID AND COMFORT... TO THE ENEMY.
HE'LL USE HER UNTIL SHE CAN'T SERVE HIM ANYMORE, THEN CUT HER DOWN. THAT'S WHAT HE DOES WITH HIS SERVANTS.
STOP CRYING, RUFUS. IT'S TIME TO BE A MAN.
I JUST WANT HIM TO GO AWAY, BUT I DON'T KNOW WHAT TO DO. THERE'S NOTHING I CAN DO.
YES, THERE IS, RUFUS. THIS IS WAR.
KILL HIM.
SLIP A KNIFE IN HIS RIBS WHILE HE'S ASLEEP. GIVE YOUR MOTHER—GIVE US ALL—A HAPPY ENDING.
SIR, NO SIR. NOT WHILE HE'S ASLEEP. THAT WOULD VIOLATE THE TERMS OF THE GENEVA CONVENTION.
ALSO, I'M NOT ALLOWED TO TOUCH THE KNIVES IN THE KITCHEN. IT'S ON THE CHALKBOARD WITH ALL MY RULES.

WHAT IS THIS STUFF, SIR?
AN INSTRUMENT PANEL THAT OPERATES A VERY OLD PUMP. IT CONTROLS THE WATER LEVEL IN THE CAVES BELOW THE HOUSE. I SAID I'D TELL YOU WHAT THIS IS ALL ABOUT. WHAT HE'S LOOKING FOR.

THE ENEMY WANTS SOMETHING THAT'S DOWN IN THOSE CAVES, RUFUS. RIGHT NOW, THEY'RE FLOODED. BUT HE CAN USE THE VALVES TO DRAIN THEM.
THERE'S A KEY—THE MOST DANGEROUS KEY OF ALL—THAT UNLOCKS A DOOR IN THAT CAVE. HE WANTS TO OPEN IT. HE WANTS WHAT'S ON THE OTHER SIDE.
RUNOFF RESERVOIR
WHAT'S ON THE OTHER SIDE, SIR?

REINFORCEMENTS.

ZACK WELLS IS CONTROLLED BY A PARASITE OF THE SPIRIT... WHAT THEY WOULD'VE CALLED A DEMON IN A LESS SCIENTIFIC AGE. IF HE COULD BRING THROUGH EVEN ONE MORE, THEY COULD MULTIPLY.
HE COULD MAKE EVERYONE IN THE WORLD LIKE HIM.

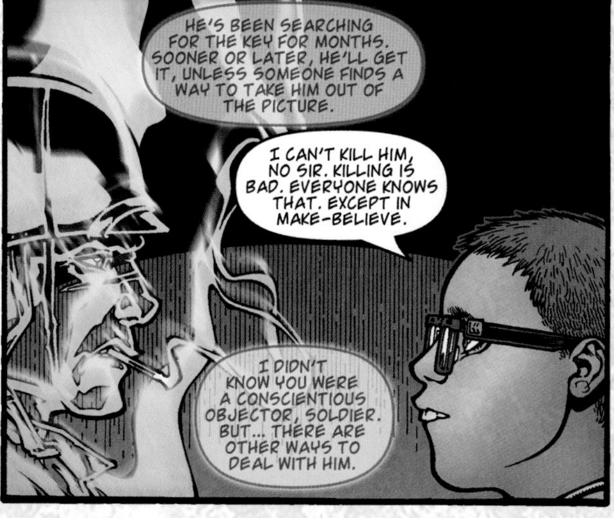
HE'S BEEN SEARCHING FOR THE KEY FOR MONTHS. SOONER OR LATER, HE'LL GET IT, UNLESS SOMEONE FINDS A WAY TO TAKE HIM OUT OF THE PICTURE.
I CAN'T KILL HIM, NO SIR. KILLING IS BAD. EVERYONE KNOWS THAT. EXCEPT IN MAKE-BELIEVE.
I DIDN'T KNOW YOU WERE A CONSCIENTIOUS OBJECTOR, SOLDIER. BUT... THERE ARE OTHER WAYS TO DEAL WITH HIM.

WHAT WAYS?

SIR? IT'S COLD, SIR.
IS IT?
I'M NOT DRESSED FOR ALL—WEATHER MANEUVERS.
WE WON'T BE OUT HERE LONG. KINSEY AND BODE ARE ALREADY LOOKING FOR YOU. THEY'RE WORRIED ABOUT YOU.
THINGS HAVE A WAY OF DISAPPEARING IN THIS HOUSE.
KEYS. CHILDREN.
I DON'T WANT TO SCARE ANYONE. I SHOULD GO BACK.
WOULDN'T IT BE SOMETHING IF WE COULD USE THIS PLACE TO MAKE ZACK WELLS DISAPPEAR?
YES, SIR. YOU SAID THERE WAS SOME WAY TO DEAL WITH HIM THAT WOULDN'T BE THE SAME AS KILLING HIM. WHAT WOULD THAT BE, SIR?
I'M LEANING AGAINST IT.
ZACK WELLS DOESN'T BELONG IN OUR WORLD. HE'S AN ECHO OF SOMEONE WHO LIVED AND DIED A LONG TIME AGO. SOMEONE INFECTED. SOMEONE EVIL.
HE WAS BROUGHT BACK TO LIFE IN THIS WELLHOUSE. AND IF HE RETURNS HERE... IF HE'S EVER DRAGGED, THROWN, OR FORCED THROUGH THIS DOOR...

"...HE'S HISTORY."

DO YOU READ ME, PRIVATE?

SIR, YES SIR.

IT'LL NEVER HAPPEN, SIR. I'M NOT TOUGH ENOUGH. I'M NOT SMART ENOUGH. I'M SORRY, SIR.

THERE'S NOTHING I CAN DO.

THERE IS, THOUGH.
YOU CAN SHARE YOUR INTEL WITH THE LOCKE KIDS. THEY'LL STOP HIM. THEY JUST NEED THE TRUTH.
IF YOU KNOW WHAT'S TRUE AND YOU DON'T ACT ON IT, RUFUS, THAT MAKES YOU HIS ACCOMPLICE.
AND BELIEVE ME, BEING HIS ACCOMPLICE ISN'T ANY SAFER THAN BEING HIS ENEMY.
TAKE IT FROM SOMEONE WHO KNOWS.
RUUUUUUFUS! WHAT ARE YOU DOING OUT HERE?
WE WERE LOOKING ALL OVER FOR YOU!
THE SERGEANT SAID IT WOULD BE ALL RIGHT. WE WERE GATHERING INTELLIGENCE. HE—
—OH. HE'S GONE NOW.
CHEEZ, I HAD TO FIGHT THE WHOLE BATTLE WITHOUT YOU.
I'M SORRY.
AH, IT'S OKAY. WE CAN FIGHT ANOTHER BATTLE ANY TIME.

WHAT ARE YOU LOOKING AT, YOU CRAZY SHIT?
IF I DIDN'T KNOW BETTER, I'D THINK YOU COULD TELL I WAS WATCHING YOU.
PHILOSOSOPHOSCOPE
BESTE TEACHER
TRUEST LOVE
USEFULLEST SOULLE
UNTRUSTWORTHIE ALLY
GRAVE HAZZARD
I DIDN'T REALLY THINK OF US AS ALLIES, RUFUS, BUT I CAN SEE YOU AS UNTRUSTWORTHY, AND THE PHILOSOPHOSCOPE DOESN'T LIE.
I'D WIPE YOU OUT, BUT I'M NOT SURE ZACK WELLS COULD STAND THE ATTENTION THAT WOULD COME HIS WAY IF YOU WOUND UP DEAD.
MAYBE I'LL JUST HAVE TO TAKE A MORE SUBTLE APPROACH.
RUFUS— UNTRUSTWORTHY ALLY. ALLY. HUH. I JUST DON'T SEE IT.
YOU GOT THAT RIGHT. IT WAS TRYING TO SHOW YOU AN UNTRUSTWORTHY ALLY—
—AND YOU JUST DIDN'T SEE IT.

THINK AGAIN, PRIVATE.
ZACK WELLS IS A DOUBLE AGENT. HE'S DANGEROUS... THE MOST DANGEROUS ENEMY WE'VE EVER FACED AND WE HAVE TO STOP HIM BEFORE...
WHAT'S UP GUYS? HATE TO INTERRUPT THE WAR, BUT WE HAVE TO GET YOU HOME, ROOF. CURFEW IN TWENTY MINUTES.

HEY, YOU. I THOUGHT COACH WHEDON WAS COMING TO GET RUFUS.
IT SEEMED LIKE A NICE NIGHT FOR A WALK, SO I SAID I'D DO IT. IT JUST STARTED SNOWING.
HAS IT? MAYBE I'LL COME LOOK. WALK YOU AND RUFUS PART OF THE WAY.
OKAY. SURE. I'D LIKE THAT.
I HAVE TO GET MY BOOTS. I'LL BE RIGHT BACK.
MEET YOU OUTSIDE.

REPORT!
WE'RE TALKING ABOUT OUR NEXT WAR. RUFUS SAYS YOU'RE THE BAD GUY.
IT'S TRUE. I AM.

WHEN WE'RE AT HOME, I'M ALWAYS THE BAD GUY. SOMEONE HAS TO BE. NOW THAT YOU KNOW THE TRUTH ABOUT ME—I'LL HAVE TO FINISH YOU.
GAKKK! NKKK! FARGLE!
WE SHOULD GO IN THE PARLOR. THERE'S MORE ROOM FOR YOU TO KILL ME THERE. BESIDES, MOM SAYS THE KITCHEN IS SWITZERLAND. NO WAR ALLOWED.

AW, I WISH, BUDDY. UNFORTUNATELY, RUFUS IS MY PRISONER, AND I'M UNDER STRICT ORDERS TO MARCH HIM BACK TO THE COMPOUND FOR A SHOWER AND BED.
OTHERWISE I'LL BE IN TROUBLE WITH COMMANDANT WHEDON. I'LL KILL YOU SOME OTHER TIME. PROMISE.
SEE YOU, KIDDO. TELL YOUR SIS I'M WAITING OUTSIDE.

BYE-BYE, ZACK. GOOD LUCK. YOU KNOW, WITH KINSEY.
THANKS, KID.

IT'S A GOOD THING I SHOWED UP WHEN I DID, RUFUS. I THINK YOU WERE ABOUT TO SAY SOMETHING RETARDED.
I MEAN, MORE RETARDED THAN USUAL.
LET'S GET SOMETHING STRAIGHT.

YOU EVER TALK TO THE LOCKE KIDS OR ANYONE ELSE ABOUT ME, THEY'LL TAKE YOUR MOTHER AWAY AND PUT HER IN JAIL AND YOU'LL NEVER SEE HER AGAIN.
I THOUGHT YOU ALREADY UNDERSTOOD THAT, OR I NEVER WOULD'VE LET YOU COME HERE.
THEY'D HAVE TO PUT YOU IN FOSTER CARE. YOUR DAD ISN'T GOING TO HELP YOU. WHY DO YOU THINK HE JOINED THE AIR FORCE?

TO GET AWAY FROM YOU.
THEY'LL PUT YOU IN A STATE HOME, WITH CRIMINALS AND DRUG USERS. YOU KNOW WHAT THOSE KIDS WOULD DO WITH A LITTLE RETARD LIKE YOU?

TEAR YOU APART.

HEY.
HEY.

AND SO... A HERO FALLS!
JACK NIFE IS GONE... BUT THE WAR GOES ON!

I'M SORRY.

SO SORRY—

—WHY? I'M THE ONE WHO—

ME, TOO—

NO. NO, NO, **NO.** I FUCKED UP. I FUCKED UP WITH YOU, AND SCOT, AND JAMAL, AND JACKIE. TRYING TO PUSH EVERYONE INTO DOING THINGS, TRYING THINGS, TAKING CHANCES—

HOLD THE GUILT FOR A MINUTE. I'M THE ONE WHO NEEDS TO APOLOGIZE.

IT'S SUCH A HUGE LEAP OF TRUST, TO LET SOMEONE INTO YOUR HEAD, AND I BLEW IT. IT'S JUST—YOU KNOW—THERE'S SO MUCH ***YOU*** DON'T TELL ME. SO MUCH I ***DON'T*** KNOW.

LIKE THIS KEY TYLER IS HIDING. IT'S DANGEROUS, ISN'T IT? BUT YOU WON'T TELL ME ANYTHING ABOUT IT, WON'T LET ME HELP...

THAT STOPS TODAY. TY HASN'T EVEN TOLD ***ME*** WHERE HE'S HIDING THE OMEGA KEY.
BUT I'LL FIND OUT, AND WHEN I KNOW, ***YOU'LL*** KNOW. IT'S TOO MUCH FOR ONE KID TO DEAL WITH ANYWAY. HE ***NEEDS*** US.
AND I NEED ***YOU***. I LOVE YOU. AND I'M NOT AFRAID TO SAY IT.

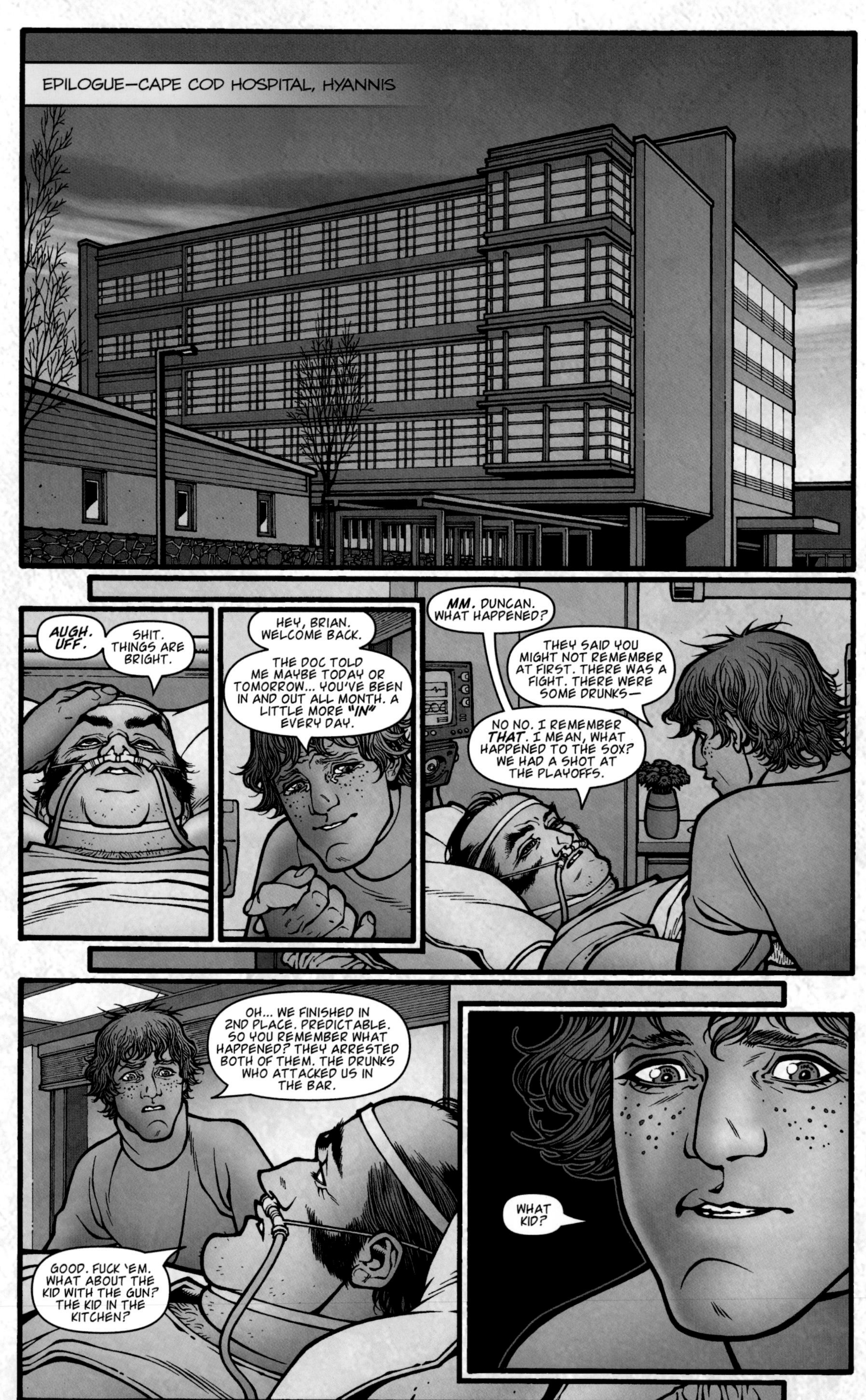
EPILOGUE—CAPE COD HOSPITAL, HYANNIS
AUGH. UFF.
SHIT. THINGS ARE BRIGHT.
HEY, BRIAN. WELCOME BACK.
THE DOC TOLD ME MAYBE TODAY OR TOMORROW... YOU'VE BEEN IN AND OUT ALL MONTH. A LITTLE MORE "IN" EVERY DAY.
MM. DUNCAN. WHAT HAPPENED?
THEY SAID YOU MIGHT NOT REMEMBER AT FIRST. THERE WAS A FIGHT. THERE WERE SOME DRUNKS—
NO NO. I REMEMBER THAT. I MEAN, WHAT HAPPENED TO THE SOX? WE HAD A SHOT AT THE PLAYOFFS.
OH... WE FINISHED IN 2ND PLACE. PREDICTABLE. SO YOU REMEMBER WHAT HAPPENED? THEY ARRESTED BOTH OF THEM. THE DRUNKS WHO ATTACKED US IN THE BAR.
GOOD. FUCK 'EM. WHAT ABOUT THE KID WITH THE GUN? THE KID IN THE KITCHEN?
WHAT KID?

- KEYS TO THE KINGDOM -

Chapter Five

DETECTIVES

Part I

CAPE COD HOSPITAL, HYANNIS—6 DAYS AGO

SO WHAT WAS IT LIKE? BEING IN A COMA?

I DON'T KNOW.

I DON'T REMEMBER ANYTHING ABOUT IT.

IT'S LIKE I WAS A TV. SOMEONE SWITCHED ME OFF IN SEPTEMBER, TURNED ME BACK ON IN FEBRUARY.

GOOD. I MEAN—NOT GOOD. BUT BETTER THAT THAN BAD DREAMS OR... BEING IN PAIN OR SOMETHING.
I GUESS NOT FEELING ANYTHING—JUST, YOU KNOW, OBLIVION—SOMETIMES IS FOR THE BEST.

ARE YOU OKAY, KIDDO? TRY NOT TO SOUND SO TURNED ON BY THE IDEA OF OBLIVION.
WHAT'S THE HARDEST YOU'VE EVER BEEN LET DOWN?
PROBABLY WHEN THE EAGLES WENT OUT ON THEIR REUNION TOUR. FIVE HUNDRED BUCKS A TICKET AND THEY SUCKED.

HEY, KID. THE GIRL STUFF GETS BETTER AFTER HIGH SCHOOL.
REALLY?
WELL. I ASSUME. IT DIDN'T FOR ME, 'CAUSE IT TURNED OUT I WAS GAY, BUT FOR YOU IT SHOULD DEFINITELY IMPROVE.

I HAD A LOT OF DIFFICULT RELATIONSHIPS WHEN I WAS YOUR AGE. IT'S HARD TO MAKE RELATIONSHIPS WORK WITH OTHERS WHEN YOU DON'T HAVE A GOOD RELATIONSHIP WITH YOURSELF.
HEY, THAT DIDN'T SOUND TOO DOCTOR PHIL, DID IT?

MAYBE A LITTLE.
LOOK, I GOT NINE STAPLES IN MY HEAD NOW. I'M LUCKY I CAN STILL SPELL MY OWN NAME.
IF YOU CAME TO ME LOOKING FOR LITTLE NUGGETS OF WISDOM, CHECK THE BEDPAN.

I WISH YOU'D TAKE IT EASY ON YOURSELF, KIDDO.
THERE'RE TWO NASTY DRUNKS AND THEIR PSYCHO FRIEND WHO TRIED TO GET ME KILLED. IT'S NOT LIKE YOU EVER DID ANYTHING THAT GOT ANYONE KILLED.
HELL-*LLO*. A COUPLE CAPPUCCINOS FOR TYLER AND ME AND A TALL, DELICIOUSLY COLD GLASS OF PRUNE JUICE FOR YOUNG MR. ROGAN.
PRUNE JUICE. JESUS, DUNCAN, ONLY YOU COULD MAKE ME MISS MY IV DRIP.
SO DID TY TELL YOU HIS BIG NEWS? HE WAS ACCEPTED TO BERKELEY YESTERDAY.
NO SHIT. CONGRATU-FUCKING-LATIONS, TY. THAT'S WHERE YOUR PARENTS MET, ISN'T IT?
YOUR FATHER WOULD BE SO PROUD OF THE MAN YOU'RE BECOMING. OF THE CHOICES YOU'VE MADE.

I CAN'T BELIEVE IT'S GOING TO BE FIVE MORE WEEKS BEFORE I CAN BRING HIM HOME. I CAN'T BELIEVE HE'S BEEN IN THAT LITTLE HOSPITAL ROOM FIVE MONTHS.
ON THE BRIGHT SIDE, THOSE BRAINLESS BITCHES WHO RAN HIM DOWN ARE GOING TO BE IN A LITTLE ROOM FOR FIVE YEARS, RIGHT?
BALANCE.
THEY COULD HAVE HALF THAT IF THEY'D MAKE A DEAL, TELL US ABOUT THE GUY WHO CAME IN THE HOUSE WITH A GUN. BUT THEY'RE PLAYING STUPID.
I'M SURPRISED THE COPS CAN'T FIND HIM BASED ON BRIAN'S DESCRIPTION.
ACH. THERE'RE A THOUSAND DUDES ON CAPE COD WHO LOOK LIKE THE GUY BRIAN SAW. BLACK HAIR. EARLY TWENTIES—MAYBE A TEENAGER EVEN. NOSE RING.
YEAH, BUT STILL. IT'S GOT TO BE SOMEONE THE GIRLS KNEW. A BOYFRIEND OR SOMEONE. A NOSE RING, THAT'S A PRETTY DISTINCTIVE DETAIL.
NOPE. DOESN'T MATCH ANY OF THEIR RELATIVES OR FRIENDS OR—YOU KNOW, I THINK IT WAS A LIP RING, ACTUALLY.
YEAH, THAT'S WHAT BRIAN SAID. RING IN HIS LOWER LIP.
OH, WELL. IT'S OUT OF OUR HANDS. NOT LIKE WE CAN TRACK THE GUY DOWN. WHAT ARE WE, DETECTIVES?

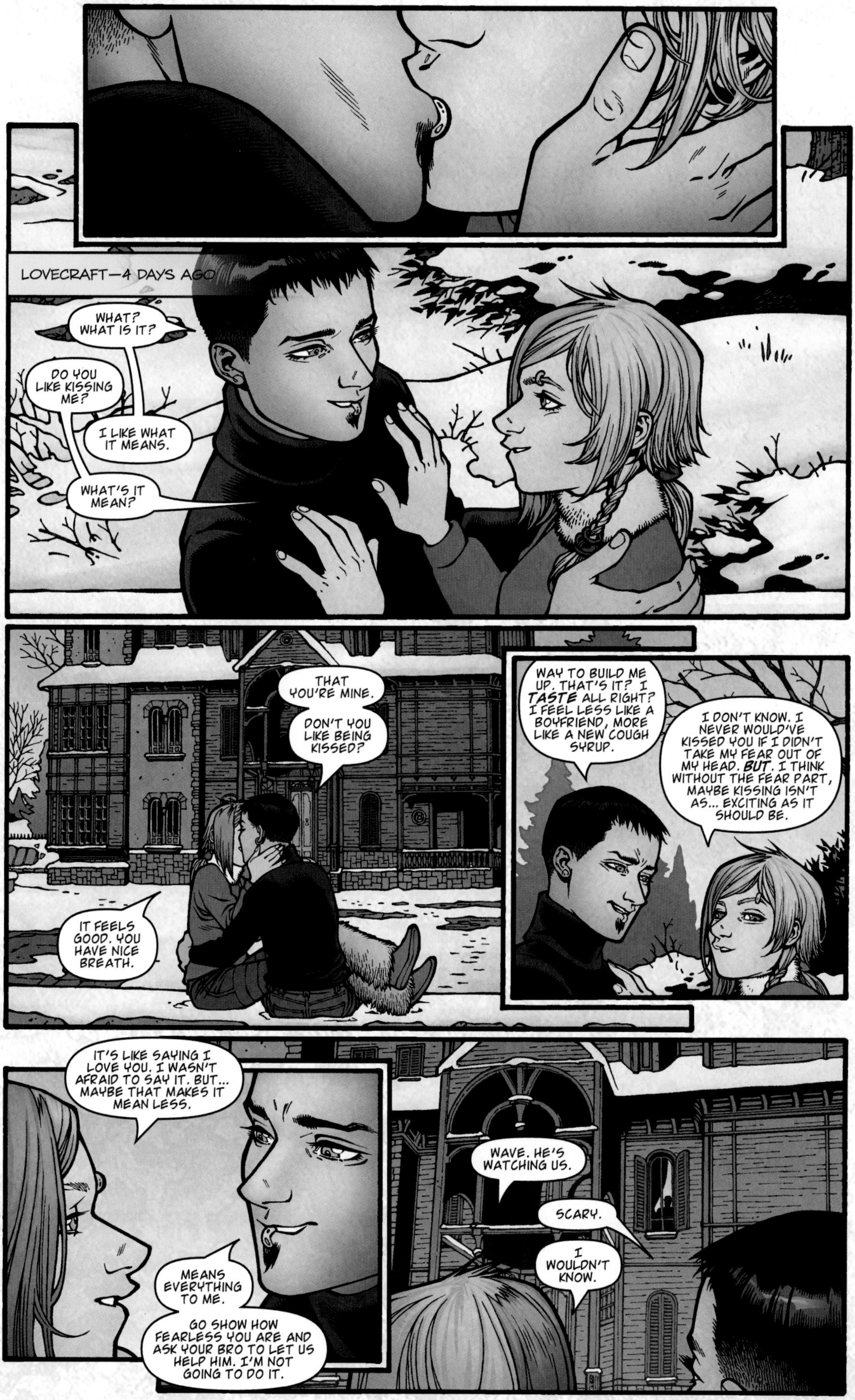

LOVECRAFT—4 DAYS AGO

WHAT? WHAT IS IT?

DO YOU LIKE KISSING ME?

I LIKE WHAT IT MEANS.

WHAT'S IT MEAN?

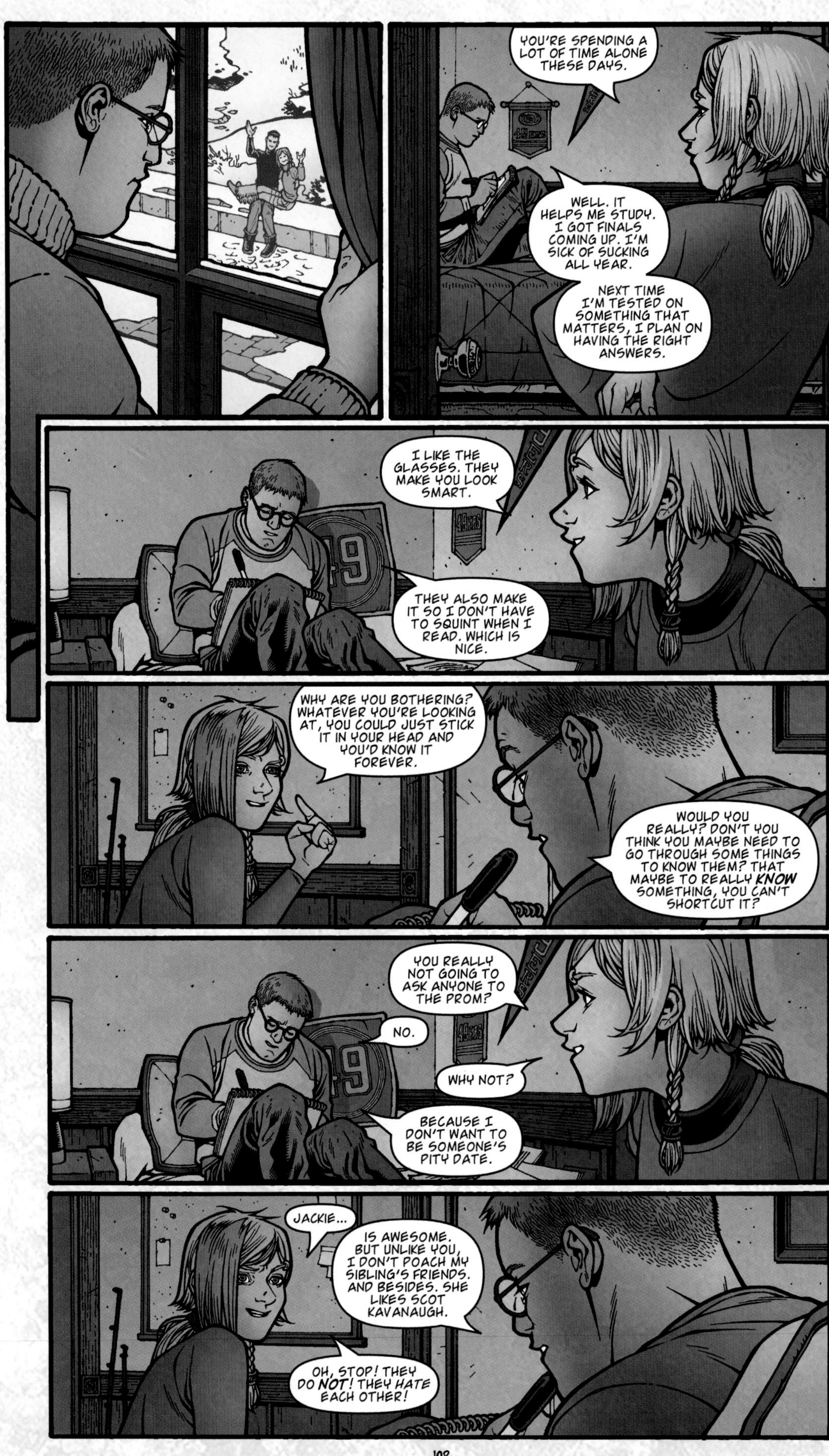
YOU'RE SPENDING A LOT OF TIME ALONE THESE DAYS.
WELL. IT HELPS ME STUDY. I GOT FINALS COMING UP. I'M SICK OF SUCKING ALL YEAR.
NEXT TIME I'M TESTED ON SOMETHING THAT MATTERS, I PLAN ON HAVING THE RIGHT ANSWERS.
I LIKE THE GLASSES. THEY MAKE YOU LOOK SMART.
THEY ALSO MAKE IT SO I DON'T HAVE TO SQUINT WHEN I READ. WHICH IS NICE.
WHY ARE YOU BOTHERING? WHATEVER YOU'RE LOOKING AT, YOU COULD JUST STICK IT IN YOUR HEAD AND YOU'D KNOW IT FOREVER.
WOULD YOU REALLY? DON'T YOU THINK YOU MAYBE NEED TO GO THROUGH SOME THINGS TO KNOW THEM? THAT MAYBE TO REALLY KNOW SOMETHING, YOU CAN'T SHORTCUT IT?
YOU REALLY NOT GOING TO ASK ANYONE TO THE PROM?
NO.
WHY NOT?
BECAUSE I DON'T WANT TO BE SOMEONE'S PITY DATE.
JACKIE...
IS AWESOME. BUT UNLIKE YOU, I DON'T POACH MY SIBLING'S FRIENDS. AND BESIDES. SHE LIKES SCOT KAVANAUGH.
OH, STOP! THEY DO NOT! THEY HATE EACH OTHER!

SHIT. RIGHT IN FRONT OF MY FACE.
STILL. YOU SHOULD... NOT BE ALONE. ON A BIG NIGHT. YOU HAVE THESE WALLS UP. TO PROTECT YOURSELF. TO PROTECT EVERYONE ELSE.
YOU DON'T HAVE TO DEAL WITH EVERYTHING ALONE. YOU DON'T HAVE TO BE ALONE.

WHERE YOU GOING WITH THIS, KINSEY?
YOU'RE THE ONLY ONE THAT KNOWS WHERE THE OMEGA KEY IS. THE DARK LADY SEEMS TO KNOW IT, TOO. THAT'S WHY **ALL** HER ATTACKS CENTER ON YOU. LET ME HELP.
I COULD HAVE A TURN HIDING IT. ZACK COULD HAVE A TURN—
WHAT'S ZACK GOT TO DO WITH IT?
HE **CARES** ABOUT YOU. THAT'S WHAT HE HAS TO DO WITH IT.
DID **HE** ASK ABOUT HELPING OUT WITH THE OMEGA KEY?
NO. YES. I DON'T KNOW. I THINK I SUGGESTED IT. THAT'S NOT THE POINT. THE POINT IS, HE'S READY TO HELP. HE **WANTS** TO HELP.

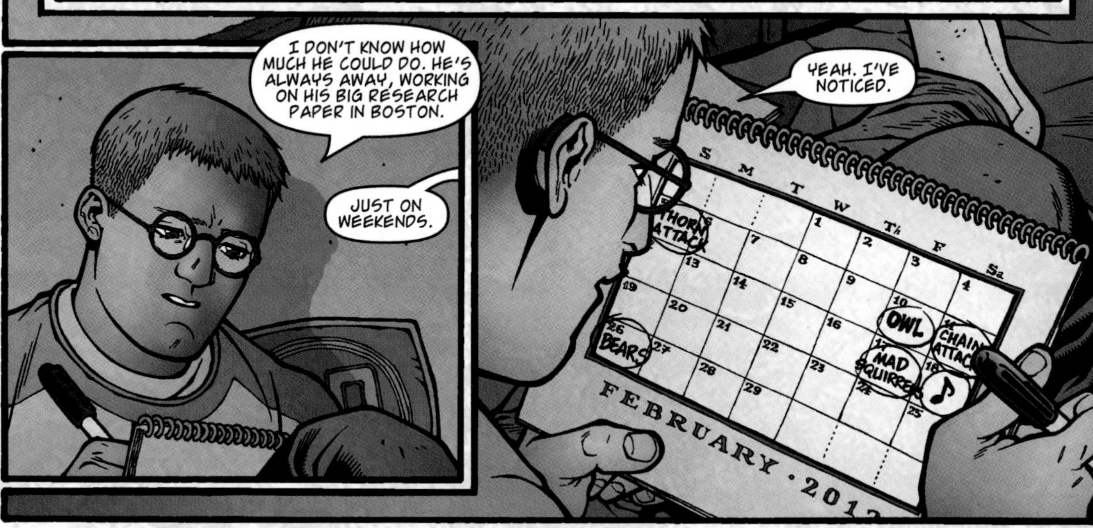
I DON'T KNOW HOW MUCH HE COULD DO. HE'S ALWAYS AWAY, WORKING ON HIS BIG RESEARCH PAPER IN BOSTON.
YEAH. I'VE NOTICED.
JUST ON WEEKENDS.
FEBRUARY · 201

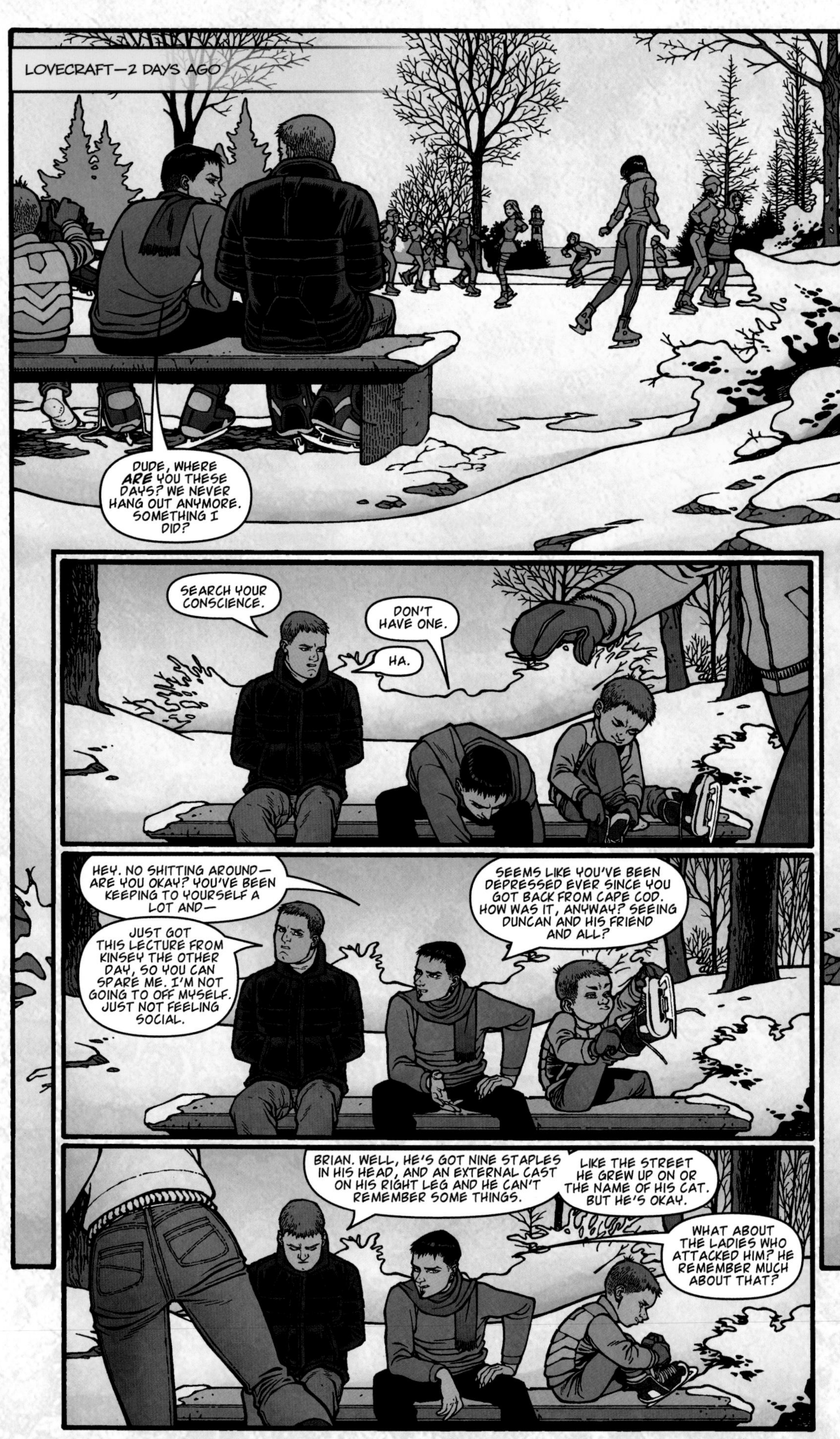
LOVECRAFT—2 DAYS AGO
DUDE, WHERE ARE YOU THESE DAYS? WE NEVER HANG OUT ANYMORE. SOMETHING I DID?
SEARCH YOUR CONSCIENCE.
DON'T HAVE ONE.
HA.
HEY. NO SHITTING AROUND—ARE YOU OKAY? YOU'VE BEEN KEEPING TO YOURSELF A LOT AND—
JUST GOT THIS LECTURE FROM KINSEY THE OTHER DAY, SO YOU CAN SPARE ME. I'M NOT GOING TO OFF MYSELF. JUST NOT FEELING SOCIAL.
SEEMS LIKE YOU'VE BEEN DEPRESSED EVER SINCE YOU GOT BACK FROM CAPE COD. HOW WAS IT, ANYWAY? SEEING DUNCAN AND HIS FRIEND AND ALL?
BRIAN. WELL, HE'S GOT NINE STAPLES IN HIS HEAD, AND AN EXTERNAL CAST ON HIS RIGHT LEG AND HE CAN'T REMEMBER SOME THINGS.
LIKE THE STREET HE GREW UP ON OR THE NAME OF HIS CAT. BUT HE'S OKAY.
WHAT ABOUT THE LADIES WHO ATTACKED HIM? HE REMEMBER MUCH ABOUT THAT?

NO.
I SPENT ALL WINTER ON ICE SKATES AND IT SUCKED. TELL ME WHY WE'RE HERE AGAIN?
TO LOOK AT GIRLS IN THEIR LITTLE SKIRTS. CHECK OUT STRAWBERRY THERE. THE REDHEAD.
YOU'RE DATING MY SISTER. SHOW SOME CLASS.
I'LL TRY. I JUST GOT A LOT OF DOG IN ME.
HALF WOLF?
DEFINITELY. HEY, BODE, LET ME—
I LOVE THIS. IT'S LIKE FLYING. IT'S LIKE BEING DEAD AGAIN. LIKE BEING A GHOST. I WAS A GHOST ONCE, YOU KNOW? I MISS BEING DEAD. IT WAS REALLY FUN.
AW, KID. YOU'RE A SCREAM.

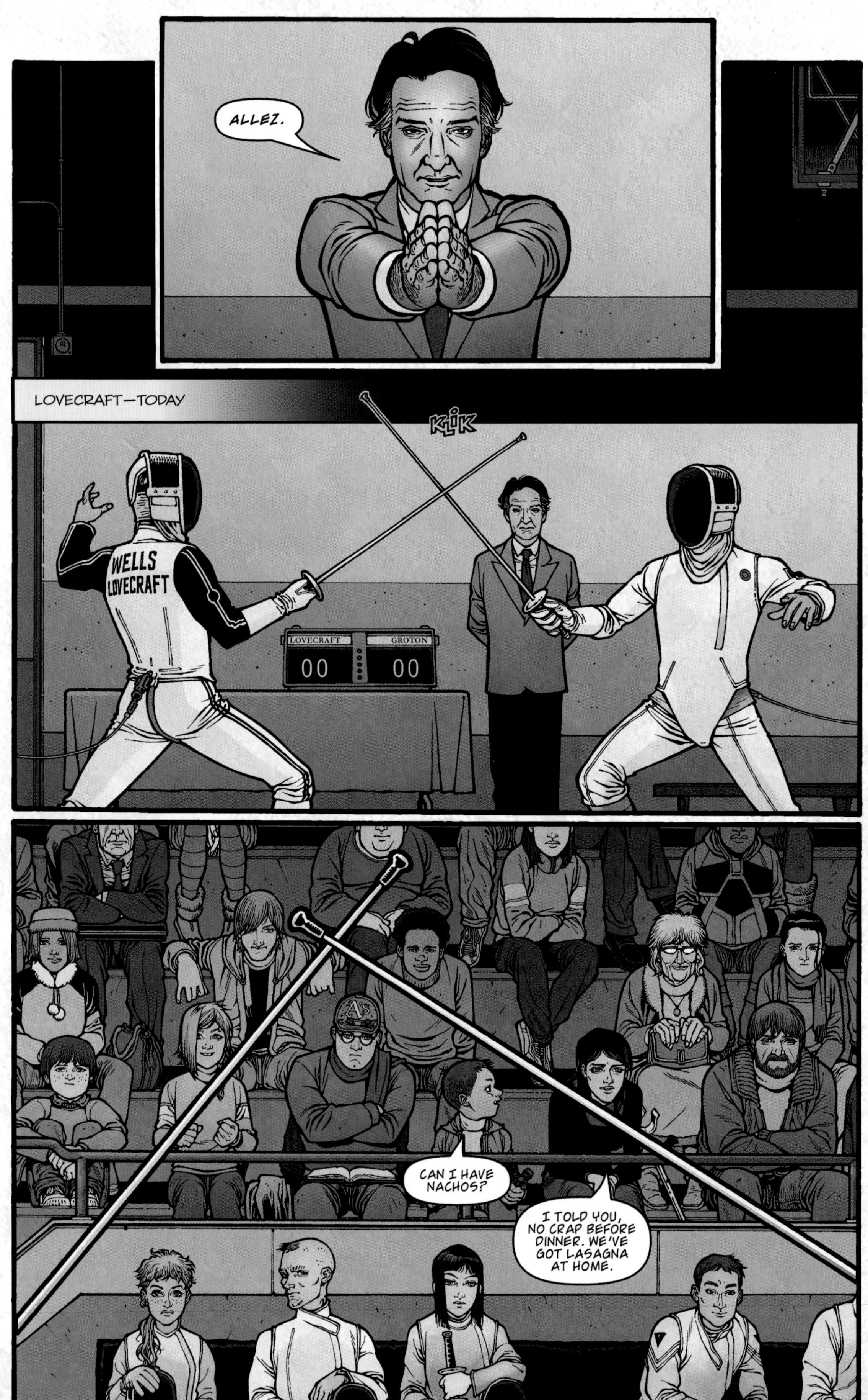
ALLEZ.
LOVECRAFT—TODAY
KLIK
WELLS
LOVECRAFT
LOVECRAFT
GROTON
00
00
CAN I HAVE NACHOS?
I TOLD YOU, NO CRAP BEFORE DINNER. WE'VE GOT LASAGNA AT HOME.

MANUGIAN
GROTON
LOVECRAFT
GROTON
01
00
YES!
I DON'T LIKE LAZYANYA. IT'S HARD TO PRONOUNCE AND IT ALWAYS BURNS MY MOUTH.
TOO BAD WE DON'T SCORE EXTRA POINTS FOR SHOWING OFF.
LOVECRAFT
MANUGIAN
LOVECRAFT
GROTON
02
00
CAN I HAVE COTTON CANDY? COTTON CANDY ISN'T FILLING.
COTTON CANDY IS JUNK.

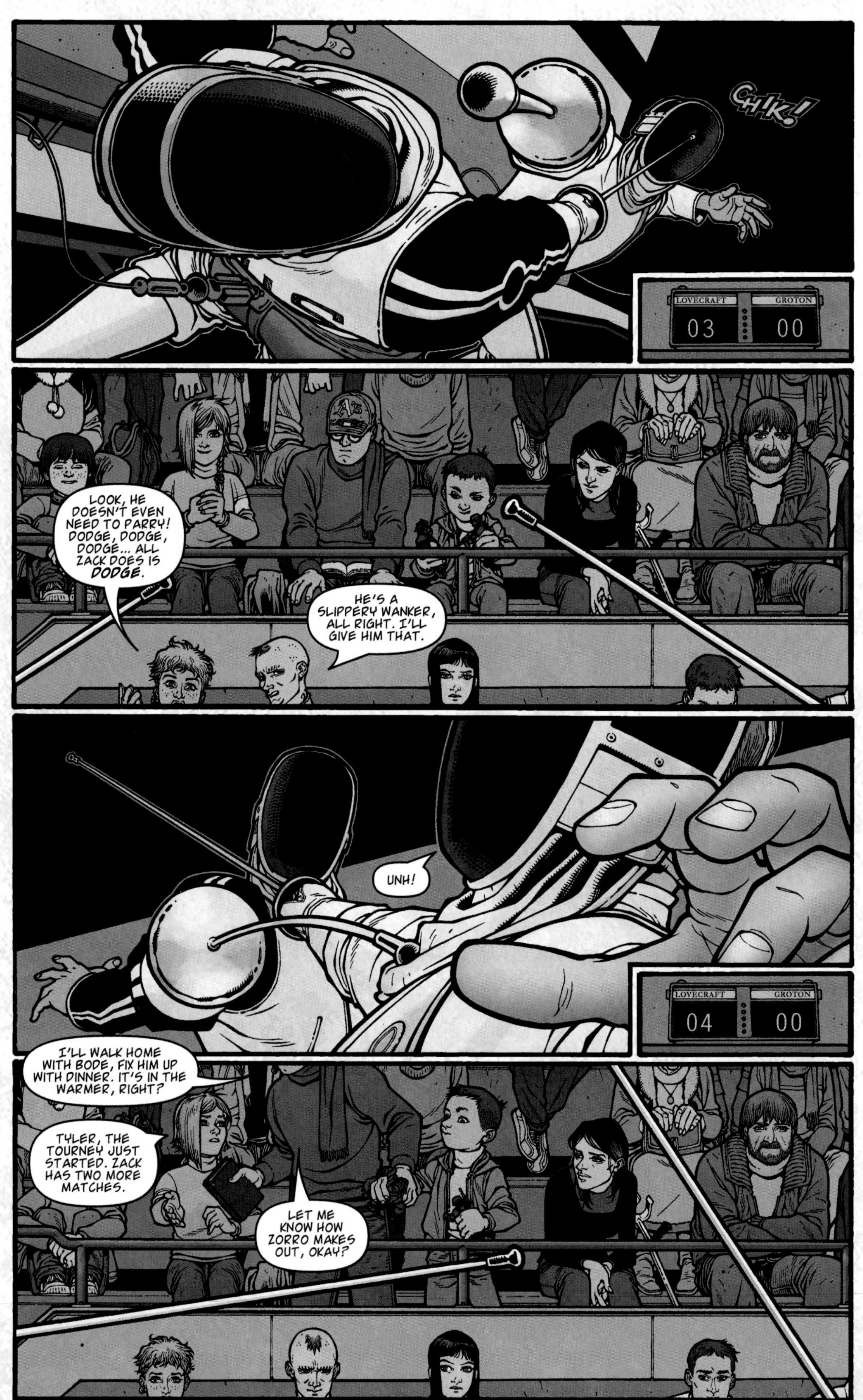
CHIK!
LOVECRAFT
GROTON
03
00
LOOK, HE DOESN'T EVEN NEED TO PARRY! DODGE, DODGE, DODGE... ALL ZACK DOES IS DODGE.
HE'S A SLIPPERY WANKER, ALL RIGHT. I'LL GIVE HIM THAT.
UNH!
LOVECRAFT
GROTON
04
00
I'LL WALK HOME WITH BODE, FIX HIM UP WITH DINNER. IT'S IN THE WARMER, RIGHT?
TYLER, THE TOURNEY JUST STARTED. ZACK HAS TWO MORE MATCHES.
LET ME KNOW HOW ZORRO MAKES OUT, OKAY?

LOVECRAFT
GROTON
05
00
HEY, TY! TY! I WAS WONDERING SOMETHING!
YEAH?
DO YOU THINK YOU CAN TEACH A MONKEY TO KUNG FU? THEY TAUGHT ONE SIGN LANGUAGE, I SAW IT ON DISCOVERY.
ALSO, MY FRIEND JAY SAYS THEY SENT A CHIMPANZEE INTO OUTER SPACE, AND I WAS WONDERING—IS HE STILL THERE? WHAT'S HE DOING UP THERE?
WHERE ARE WE?
THIS IS WHERE ZACK AND RUFUS LIVE. YOU SHOULD GIVE RUFUS HIS BUSTED ACTION FIGURE BACK.
93
COME ON IN! DOOR'S OPEN!
TYLER!
HI, MRS. WHEDON.

WE WERE IN THE NEIGHBORHOOD AND RUFUS LEFT HIS ACTION FIGURE AT OUR HOUSE. IT'S KIND OF BUSTED UP, BUT WE FIGURED HE MIGHT WANT IT BACK.

HE'LL BE GLAD TO SEE GOOD OL' JACK NIFE. THAT'S ONE OF HIS FAVORITES.

I JUST MADE COOKIES. THEY'RE STILL HOT.

CAN I HAVE ONE?

DON'T TELL MOM I LET YOU.

MA'AM? I ALSO FORGOT TO COPY DOWN THE ETHICS READING. CAN I RUN UP TO ZACK'S ROOM AND CHECK HIS NOTEBOOK?

OH, I DON'T SEE WHY NOT.

BODE, DO YOU WANT TO BRING RUFUS HIS ACTION FIGURE AND A COOKIE?

YES, MA'AM.

HEY, UH... MISS WHEDON? I JUST WANTED TO SAY, IT'S PRETTY COOL YOU AGREED TO LET YOUR NEPHEW STAY WITH YOU ALL YEAR.

I GUESS YOU AND ZACK HAVE A REAL SPECIAL RELATIONSHIP.

WE SURE DO.
HOW'D YOU TWO GET SO CLOSE? DID YOU VISIT HIM IN TEXAS MUCH? IT'S HARD TO IMAGINE HIM AS A LITTLE GUY.
IT SURE IS.
WHAT WAS HE LIKE AS A LITTLE BOY? WAS HE ALWAYS A SWEET-TALKER, OR DID THAT HAPPEN LATER?
ARE YOU SURE YOU DON'T WANT A COOKIE YOURSELF, TY?
NO, THANK YOU, MA'AM.

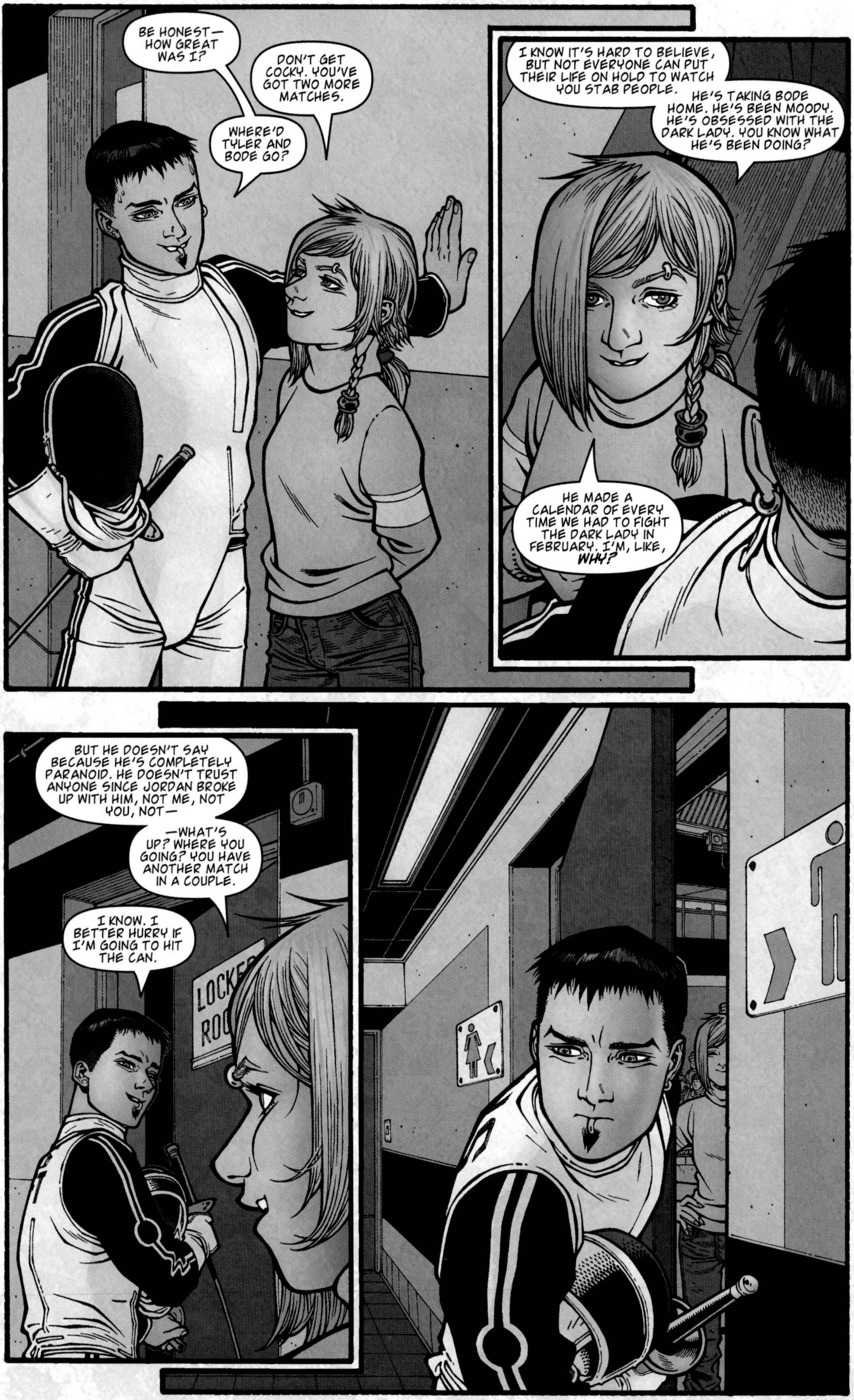

BE HONEST—HOW GREAT WAS I?

DON'T GET COCKY. YOU'VE GOT TWO MORE MATCHES.

WHERE'D TYLER AND BODE GO?

I KNOW IT'S HARD TO BELIEVE, BUT NOT EVERYONE CAN PUT THEIR LIFE ON HOLD TO WATCH YOU STAB PEOPLE.

HE'S TAKING BODE HOME. HE'S BEEN MOODY. HE'S OBSESSED WITH THE DARK LADY. YOU KNOW WHAT HE'S BEEN DOING?

HE MADE A CALENDAR OF EVERY TIME WE HAD TO FIGHT THE DARK LADY IN FEBRUARY. I'M, LIKE, ***WHY?***

BUT HE DOESN'T SAY BECAUSE HE'S COMPLETELY PARANOID. HE DOESN'T TRUST ANYONE SINCE JORDAN BROKE UP WITH HIM, NOT ME, NOT YOU, NOT—

—WHAT'S UP? WHERE YOU GOING? YOU HAVE ANOTHER MATCH IN A COUPLE.

I KNOW. I BETTER HURRY IF I'M GOING TO HIT THE CAN.

LOCKER ROOM

HEY—HI, RUFUS. I—WELL, BODE— FOUND YOUR ACTION GUY. JACK NIFE. I GUESS YOU LEFT HIM AT OUR HOUSE. SORRY HE GOT BROKE.
THANK YOU, SIR.
WHAT HAPPENED TO HIM ANYWAY?
THE ENEMY AMBUSHED HIM.
THAT'S WHAT HAPPENS IN WAR. PEOPLE GET KILLED.
PERMISSION TO SPEAK FREELY, SIR.
PERMISSION GRANTED.
THIS HOUSE ISN'T SAFE, SIR. YOU'RE IN ENEMY TERRITORY. I WOULD RETREAT.
STAY WITH RUFUS, BODE. I'LL BE RIGHT BACK.

I DON'T GET IT. I DON'T UNDERSTAND WHAT GOT YOU LOOKING MY WAY.
I WAS SO CAREFUL AND— NO OFFENSE, TY— YOU AREN'T EXACTLY SHERLOCK HOLMES.
BALLS.
THAT'S THE BEST YOU GOT? BALLS?
SEE, THIS IS WHAT I MEAN. YOUR DAD WAS A THINKER. BUT YOU'RE JUST A DUMBASS JOCK. EVEN YOUR INSULTS ARE DUMBASS.
CLIC

I'M NOT INSULTING YOU. I'M ANSWERING YOUR QUESTION ABOUT WHAT GOT ME LOOKING YOUR WAY.
YOU ATTACKED US IN THE WOODS AS A DOG AND WHEN I WAS WRESTLING YOU OFF ME, I NOTICED YOU HAD NUTS.
IT GOT ME THINKING THAT IF THERE'S A KEY TO CHANGE YOU INTO AN ANIMAL, OR TO CHANGE YOUR SIZE, THERE MIGHT BE ONE TO CHANGE YOUR GENDER.
SO I STARTED THINKING, WHAT IF THE DARK LADY IS ACTUALLY A DARK GUY?

DON'T MOVE.

...DON'T MOVE DON'T MOVE, DON'T MOVE ALONG... STAY WHERE YOU ARE, THIS IS THE "DON'T MOVE" SONG...

YOU CAN TALK IF YOU WANT. I'M SURE YOU HAVE SOME THINGS TO SAY.
WHY DON'T YOU START BY TELLING ME WHERE THE OMEGA KEY IS?
...YOU CAN TALK, YOU CAN TALK, WE CAN HAVE A LITTLE CHAT... ...AS LONG AS YOU SAY WHERE THE OMEGA KEY IS AT...
NICE TRY, BUT I USED MY HEAD FOR ONCE. THAT THING CAN SING ALL IT WANTS, YOU'RE STILL NOT GOING TO GET WHAT YOU WANT OUT OF ME.
I WAS WONDERING WHAT HAPPENED TO THE MUSIC BOX. THAT THING ALMOST GOT ME AND BODE KILLED.
WELLS
LOVECRAFT
WELL, IF AT FIRST YOU DON'T SUCCEED AND ALL THAT.
I'M NOT QUITE SURE WHY THE MUSIC WON'T MAKE YOU SPILL THE BEANS. EVERYONE DANCES AND SINGS TO THE MUSIC.
BUT IF YOU WON'T TELL ME EASY, TY, I'M COMFORTABLE WITH CUTTING THE TRUTH OUT OF YOU.
WHAT, WITH YOUR TOURNAMENT FOIL? HAVE FUN, THAT THING WOULDN'T CUT THROUGH—
AA!
NO, THIS IS MY OTHER SWORD. THE ONE WITH THE SHARP TIP. I LEFT MY TOURNAMENT FOIL BACK AT THE GYM.
YOU KNOW I WAS A TERRIBLE FENCER UNTIL I USED THE HEAD KEY TO LEARN THE MOVES OF THE GREATS. I STUCK A VIDEOTAPE IN MY HEAD. EVERYONE USED VIDEOTAPE THEN.

CHONG CHANG CHONG
DON'T MAKE ME POP YOUR EYEBALL OUT.
SOUNDS LIKE SOMEONE'S HERE. YOU GOING TO CUT ME UP WHILE YOU'VE GOT VISITORS?
DON'T MOVE.

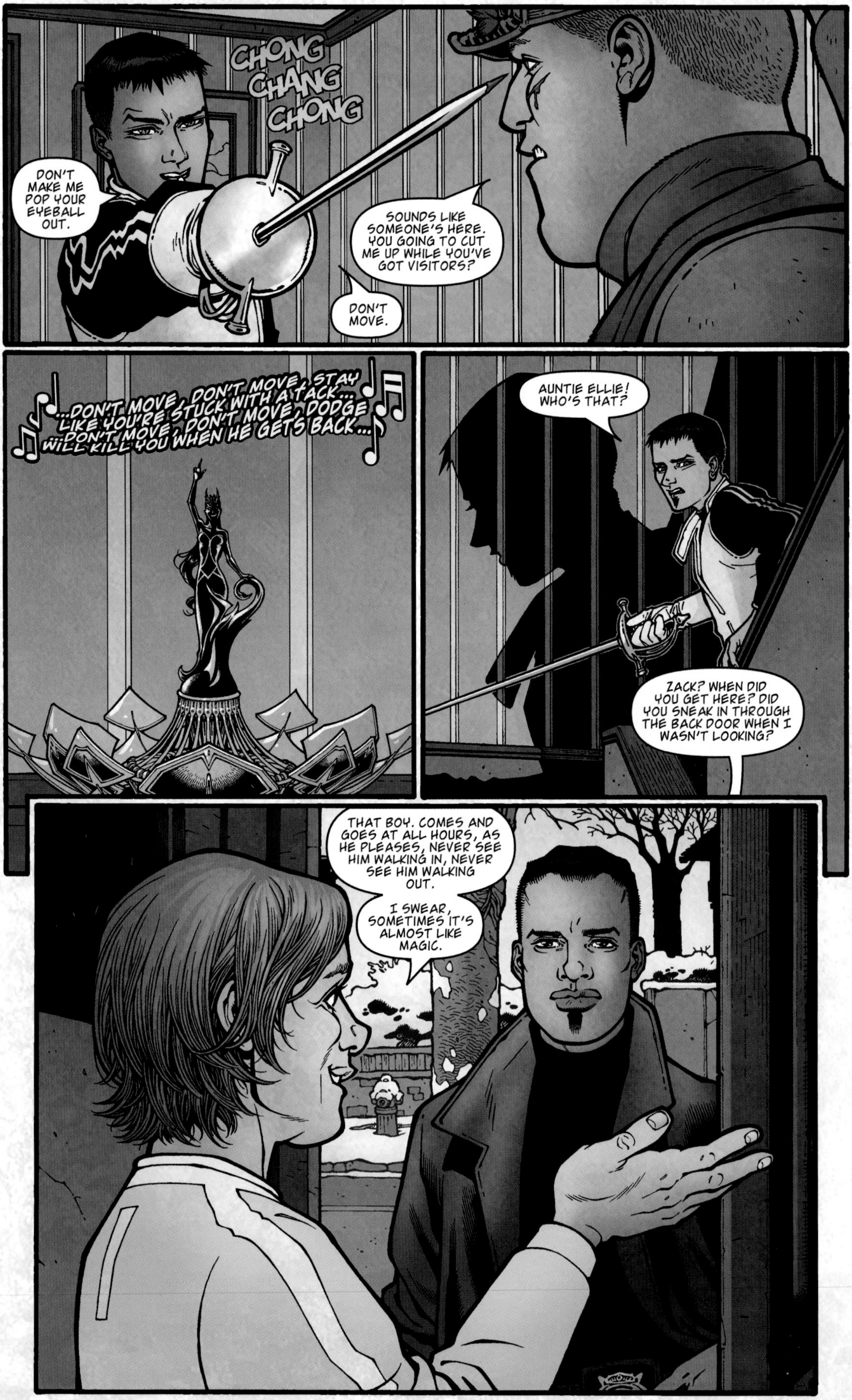

...DON'T MOVE, DON'T MOVE, STAY LIKE YOU'RE STUCK WITH A TACK... ...DON'T MOVE, DON'T MOVE, DODGE WILL KILL YOU WHEN HE GETS BACK...

AUNTIE ELLIE! WHO'S THAT?
ZACK? WHEN DID YOU GET HERE? DID YOU SNEAK IN THROUGH THE BACK DOOR WHEN I WASN'T LOOKING?

THAT BOY. COMES AND GOES AT ALL HOURS, AS HE PLEASES, NEVER SEE HIM WALKING IN, NEVER SEE HIM WALKING OUT.
I SWEAR, SOMETIMES IT'S ALMOST LIKE MAGIC.

Part II

CHARGE.
NO! PLEASE!

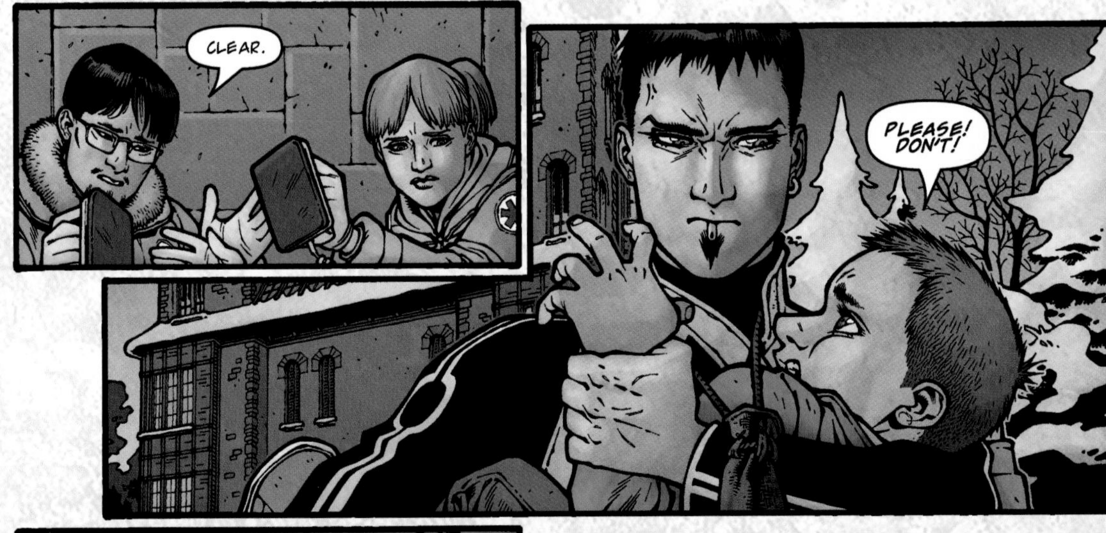
CLEAR.
PLEASE! DON'T!

IS HE DEAD?
SHUT UP.
THIS WILL BE OVER SOON.

LOVECRAFT—FIVE DAYS AGO
THERE SHE IS AGAIN.
HM? THERE WHO IS?

ELLIE WHEDON. TRACK COACH OVER AT THE ACADEMY.
SHE COMES OUT AND LIGHTS THE MEMORY CANDLES FOR HIM EVERY NIGHT.

FOOLISH TO THINK ANYONE WOULD BELIEVE IT WAS SUICIDE. IF HE WAS GOING TO KILL HIMSELF, HE WOULD'VE USED THOSE PILLS AND THE ABUNDANT ALCOHOL AT HAND.
SO MUCH MORE PEACEFUL THAN THE GUN.

THEY OUGHT TO HAVE FUNERALS FOR TEACHERS LIKE THEY HAVE FUNERALS FOR COPS, DON'T YOU THINK? PUT ON A SHOW.
YOU KNOW HOW COPS GET A RIFLE SALUTE? TEACHERS OUGHT TO HAVE SOMETHING.
THEY COULD PASS OUT A MULTIPLE CHOICE TEST AT THE MEMORIAL SERVICE. YOU HAVE TO FILL IT OUT WITH A NUMBER TWO PENCIL, SHOW WHAT YOU REMEMBER ABOUT THE DECEASED.
INSTEAD, ALL THIS GUY GETS IS EIGHT LOUSY CANDLES AND ONE DEPRESSED TRACK COACH. TEACHERS HAVE A SHIT DEAL.

YOU SEE ANYTHING YOU DIDN'T SEE ALL THE OTHER TIMES WE'VE BEEN IN HERE?
NO. AND TOMORROW, JOSEPH RIDGEWAY'S OLDEST SON WILL COME AND PACK EVERYTHING AWAY AND IT WON'T BE A CRIME SCENE ANYMORE.
IT WILL BE FACULTY HOUSING. AND JOE RIDGEWAY'S MURDER WILL BE SHUFFLED AWAY INTO THE COLD CASE FILE.
SIR? IF THERE WAS ANYTHING TO FIND IN THIS ROOM, YOU WOULD'VE FOUND IT.
YOU GOT BLOOD. YOU GOT DNA. YOU KNOW RIDGEWAY DIDN'T KILL HIMSELF.
THIS ROOM GAVE YOU EVERYTHING IT HAD. WHAT YOU'RE LOOKING FOR IS OUT THERE. I DON'T KNOW WHERE. BUT SOMEWHERE.
YES. I'M SURE YOU'RE RIGHT. WHAT I'M LOOKING FOR IS PROBABLY OUT THERE...
...YOU SAY SHE COMES EVERY NIGHT? WHY DO YOU THINK THAT IS? WERE THEY CLOSE?
PRETTY CLOSE, I GUESS. SHE WAS HIS STUDENT BEFORE THEY WERE TEACHERS TOGETHER. ALSO SHE MIGHT BE FEELING ESPECIALLY SENSITIVE RIGHT NOW.
HER MOTHER WAS JOE RIDGEWAY'S AGE, AND SHE JUST DIED, TOO. LAST SPRING, IN THAT ACCIDENT UP AT SOGGY COVE. RIGHT BEHIND KEYHOUSE.
WHAT ACCIDENT?

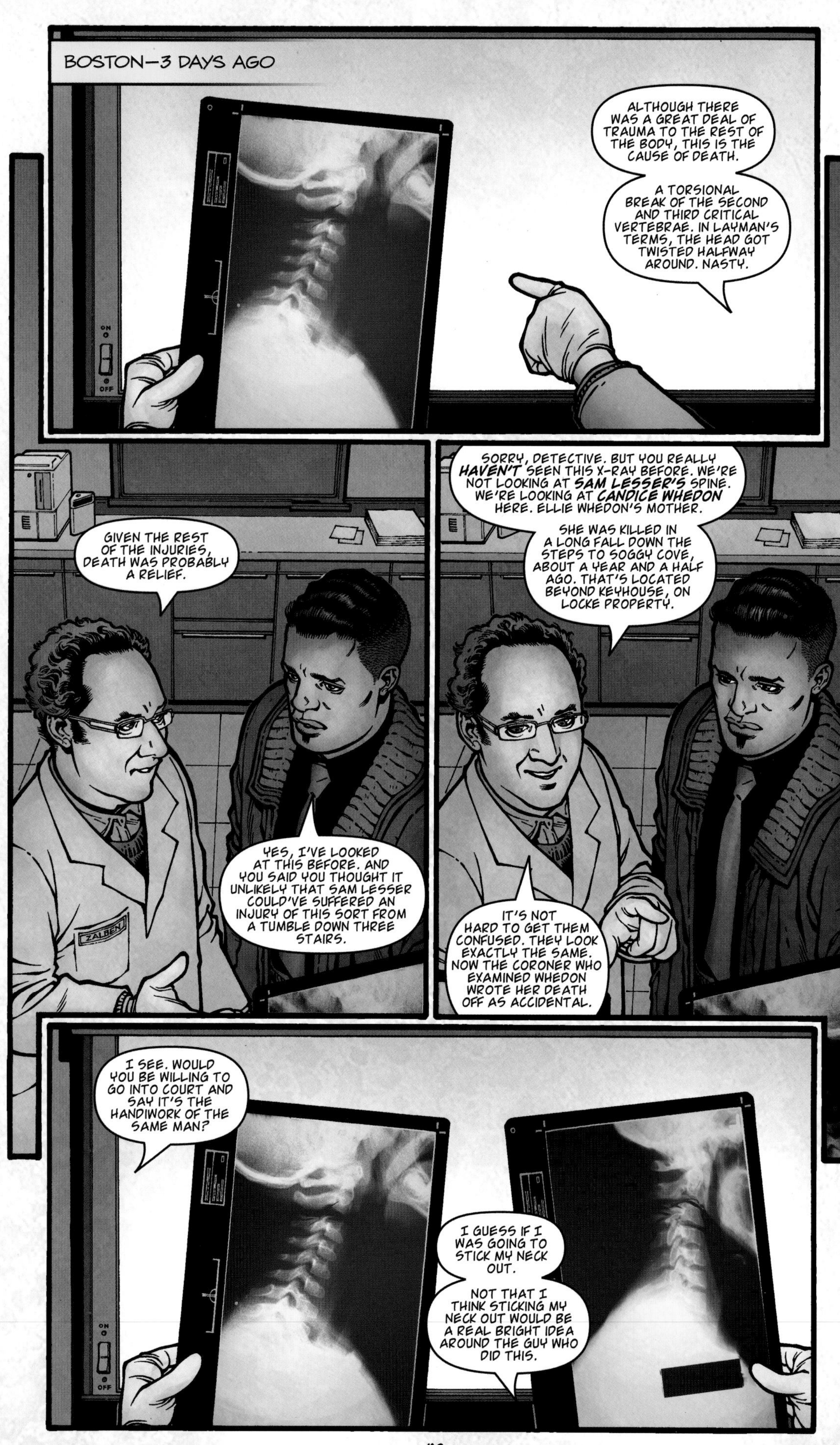
BOSTON—3 DAYS AGO
ALTHOUGH THERE WAS A GREAT DEAL OF TRAUMA TO THE REST OF THE BODY, THIS IS THE CAUSE OF DEATH.
A TORSIONAL BREAK OF THE SECOND AND THIRD CRITICAL VERTEBRAE. IN LAYMAN'S TERMS, THE HEAD GOT TWISTED HALFWAY AROUND. NASTY.
GIVEN THE REST OF THE INJURIES, DEATH WAS PROBABLY A RELIEF.
YES, I'VE LOOKED AT THIS BEFORE. AND YOU SAID YOU THOUGHT IT UNLIKELY THAT SAM LESSER COULD'VE SUFFERED AN INJURY OF THIS SORT FROM A TUMBLE DOWN THREE STAIRS.
ZALBEN
SORRY, DETECTIVE. BUT YOU REALLY **HAVEN'T** SEEN THIS X-RAY BEFORE. WE'RE NOT LOOKING AT **SAM LESSER'S** SPINE. WE'RE LOOKING AT **CANDICE WHEDON** HERE. ELLIE WHEDON'S MOTHER.
SHE WAS KILLED IN A LONG FALL DOWN THE STEPS TO SOGGY COVE, ABOUT A YEAR AND A HALF AGO. THAT'S LOCATED BEYOND KEYHOUSE, ON LOCKE PROPERTY.
IT'S NOT HARD TO GET THEM CONFUSED. THEY LOOK EXACTLY THE SAME. NOW THE CORONER WHO EXAMINED WHEDON WROTE HER DEATH OFF AS ACCIDENTAL.
I SEE. WOULD YOU BE WILLING TO GO INTO COURT AND SAY IT'S THE HANDIWORK OF THE SAME MAN?
I GUESS IF I WAS GOING TO STICK MY NECK OUT.
NOT THAT I THINK STICKING MY NECK OUT WOULD BE A REAL BRIGHT IDEA AROUND THE GUY WHO DID THIS.

REVERE, MASSACHUSETTS—1 DAY AGO
YES, IS THIS THE WHEDON RESIDENCE? MY NAME IS DETECTIVE MUTUKU, WITH THE MASSACHUSETTS STATE POLICE.
COULD I SPEAK TO YOUR MOTHER, SON?

MY MOTHER ISN'T HERE. SHE'S AT WORK. I'M AT HOME WITH ZACK.
ARE YOU GOING TO ARREST HER? ZACK SAYS IF YOU ARREST HER, I'LL HAVE TO GO TO FOSTER CARE.

YOUR MOTHER ISN'T IN TROUBLE, SON. I JUST WANTED TO TALK TO HER. WHO IS THIS ZACK PERSON? WHY WOULD HE SAY SOMETHING LIKE THAT TO YOU?

ROOF! WHO'S ON THE PHONE?
SOMEONE FOR MOM!
TELL 'EM TO CALL BACK!
ZACK SAYS I HAVE TO GO. IF HE KNEW I WAS TALKING TO A POLICEMAN HE'D BE REALLY MAD. GOODBYE.

LOVECRAFT, MASSACHUSETTS—NOW
ZACK? MR. MUTUKU WANTS TO TALK TO ME ABOUT—WELL, I DON'T KNOW WHAT ABOUT. DO YOU WANT TO GIVE US A MOMENT TO...
IT WON'T BE NECESSARY TO SPEAK PRIVATELY, MS. WHEDON. I'D LIKE TO TALK TO ZACK AS MUCH AS I'D LIKE TO TALK TO YOU.
ALL RIGHT. I HOPE NO ONE'S IN TROUBLE.
OH, NOT AT ALL. I'VE JUST BEEN INTERVIEWING PEOPLE WHO KNEW JOE RIDGEWAY. DID YOU KNOW HIM, ZACK?
YOU MEAN THE TEACHER WHO DIED, LIKE, LAST YEAR?
NO. MY GIRLFRIEND HAD A CLASS WITH HIM AND THOUGHT HE WAS A REAL SWEET OLD DUDE. SHE LIKED HIS BOW TIES. I'M SORRY I NEVER HAD A CHANCE TO GET TO KNOW HIM.
WHAT ABOUT CANDICE WHEDON? ELLIE'S MOTHER? DID YOU KNOW HER WELL, ZACK? WAS SHE A REAL SWEET OLD LADY?
YOU SHOULDN'T DO THAT, YOU KNOW?
DO WHAT?
SHAKE HANDS WITH A GUY YOU THINK MAYBE MURDERED A FEW PEOPLE. NOT WHEN HE'S HOLDING A KNIFE.

ZACK! STOP! OH, MY GOD!
ZACK? WHAT ARE YOU DOING?
IF YOU KNEW HOW GOOD THIS FELT, YOU WOULDN'T BE SURPRISED I'M DOING IT.
YOU'D BE SURPRISED I DIDN'T DO IT SOONER.

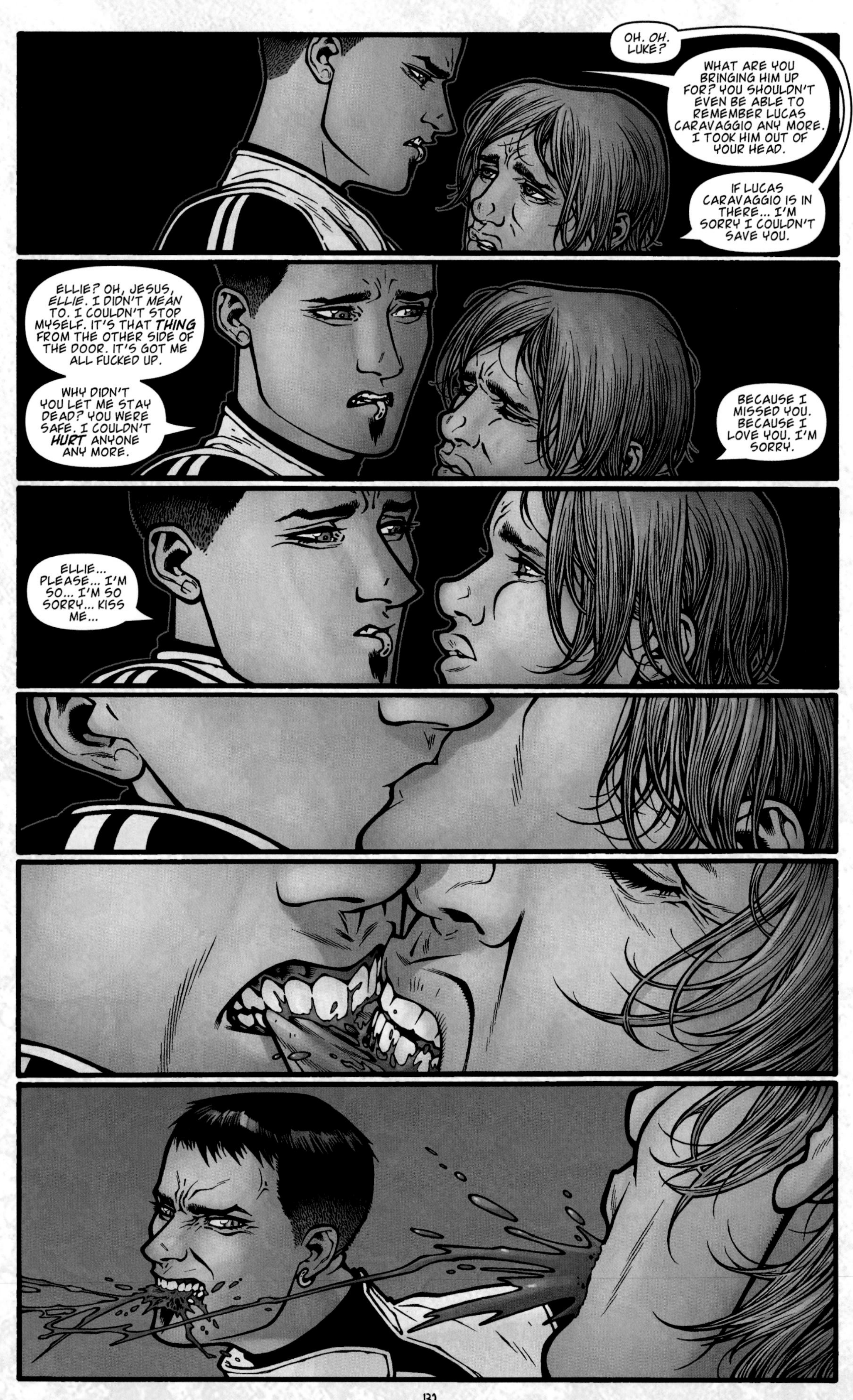
OH. OH. LUKE?
WHAT ARE YOU BRINGING HIM UP FOR? YOU SHOULDN'T EVEN BE ABLE TO REMEMBER LUCAS CARAVAGGIO ANY MORE. I TOOK HIM OUT OF YOUR HEAD.
IF LUCAS CARAVAGGIO IS IN THERE... I'M SORRY I COULDN'T SAVE YOU.
ELLIE? OH, JESUS, ELLIE. I DIDN'T MEAN TO. I COULDN'T STOP MYSELF. IT'S THAT THING FROM THE OTHER SIDE OF THE DOOR. IT'S GOT ME ALL FUCKED UP.
WHY DIDN'T YOU LET ME STAY DEAD? YOU WERE SAFE. I COULDN'T HURT ANYONE ANY MORE.
BECAUSE I MISSED YOU. BECAUSE I LOVE YOU. I'M SORRY.
ELLIE... PLEASE... I'M SO... I'M SO SORRY... KISS ME...

WHAT ARE YOU DOING?
WELLS LOVECRAFT
LET GO OF THAT.
CHAK!

PUT THE WEAPON DOWN BEFORE YOU ARE SERIOUSLY HURT, CHILD.
YOU'RE WRONG THERE. I CAN'T BE— SERIOUSLY— HURT.
PAIN IS USEFUL TO MOVE THE MEAT, IN TIMES OF DISTRESS. BUT NOT NECESSARY. I CAN TURN IT OFF IF IT GETS TOO DISTRACTING AND ISN'T PROVIDING HELPFUL INFORMATION.
IT'S JUST THAT I LIKE IT SO. I LIKE THE WAY THE MEAT FEELS. EVEN WHEN IT'S BAD, IT'S GOOD.
PUT YOUR SILLY STICKER DOWN, BOY. THIS IS NO FENCING MATCH AND I'M NOT PLAYING TO SCORE POINTS FOR MY TEAM.
PLEASE. IF YOU DO NOT SURRENDER, I WILL CRIPPLE YOU.

GET BACK.
YOU TOO, ROOF. STAND ASIDE.
THIS ISN'T COMPLICATED. EVERYONE GETS AWAY FROM ME OR I'LL KILL HIM. I'LL CUT THIS LITTLE BOY APART.

THERE'S NOWHERE TO GO, ZACK. UNLESS YOU KNOW HOW TO FLY, THERE'S NO WAY OUT FOR YOU UP THERE.

THANKS FOR THE TIP.

SON. YOU NEED TO LEAVE THIS HOUSE.
LET GO OF ME.

MOM? MOM?

BODE? IF THAT'S YOU, BODE, COVER YOUR EARS, AND DON'T LISTEN TO ANYTHING!
...DODGE IS COMING TO CUT YOU DOWN AND WATCH YOU FALL...
...DON'T MOVE, DON'T MOVE, DON'T MOVE AT ALL...
TY! TY, HELP ME!
I CAN'T, KID. I'VE GOT TO LISTEN TO THE MUSIC.
A'S
WHAT'D YOU SAY?
I SAID KEEP YOUR EARS COVERED AND DON'T LISTEN!
OKAY. OKAY!
NA NA NA NA NA NA NA...

WHAT THE HELL IS GOING ON?

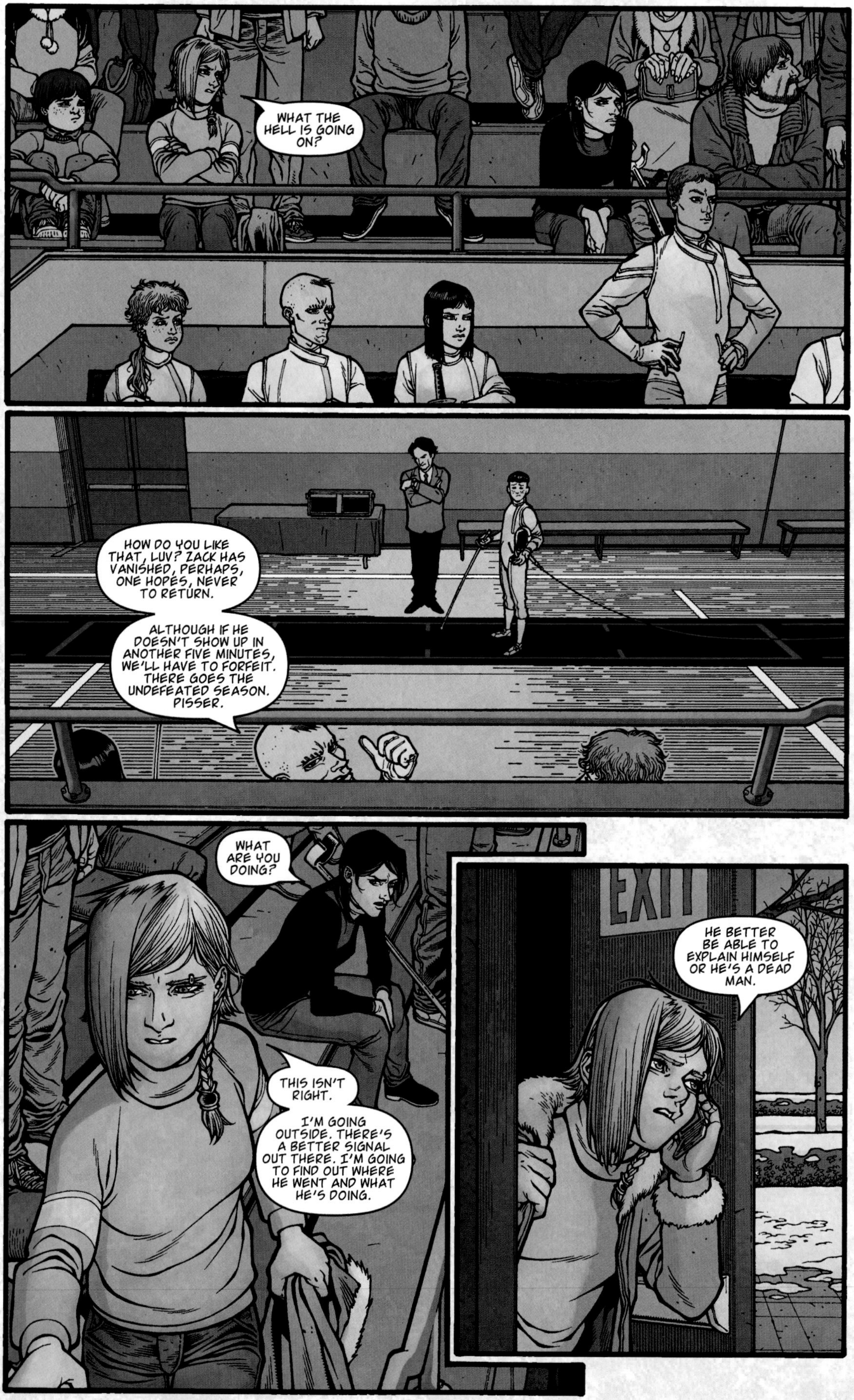

HOW DO YOU LIKE THAT, LUV? ZACK HAS VANISHED, PERHAPS, ONE HOPES, NEVER TO RETURN.
ALTHOUGH IF HE DOESN'T SHOW UP IN ANOTHER FIVE MINUTES, WE'LL HAVE TO FORFEIT. THERE GOES THE UNDEFEATED SEASON. PISSER.

WHAT ARE YOU DOING?

THIS ISN'T RIGHT.

I'M GOING OUTSIDE. THERE'S A BETTER SIGNAL OUT THERE. I'M GOING TO FIND OUT WHERE HE WENT AND WHAT HE'S DOING.

EXIT

HE BETTER BE ABLE TO EXPLAIN HIMSELF OR HE'S A DEAD MAN.

EVERYONE ON THE FLOOR AND—AHHFUCKA—!

NO, MAN, HE'S GOT MY BROTHER, HE'LL THROW HIM OUT THE WINDOW!

WHY AREN'T YOU ANSWERING YOUR DAMN CELL PHONE?
MAYBE YOU WENT HOME?
CHEEP CHEEP CHEEP
I HAVE TO ANSWER THE PHONE. I'LL COME BACK.

HELLO? OH, HI, KINSEY. ZACK?
HE JUST KILLED MY MOTHER. NOW HE'S FLYING AWAY WITH BODE.
WAIT, IT LOOKS LIKE THEY'RE LANDING.

ZACK AND BODE ARE GOING AWAY NOW. ZACK IS MAKING BODE DISAPPEAR.
93
ALL RIGHT, KINSEY. I'LL TALK TO YOU LATER. I'M GOING TO SIT WITH MY MOTHER. SHE SHOULDN'T BE ALONE.

SAM? I KNOW YOU'RE THERE. I WANT YOU TO LISTEN TO ME CLOSELY.

GGGKKKK

I'M GOING TO GIVE YOU WHAT YOU WANT. I'M GOING TO GIVE YOU MY BODY.

IT'S NOT DOING ME ANY GOOD. KINSEY LIKES ME, BUT SHE'LL NEVER GET TYLER TO TELL ME WHERE THE OMEGA KEY IS.

SO I'VE DECIDED. I'LL TAKE THE KID. THEY LOVE AND TRUST HIM. THEY TELL HIM EVERYTHING. I'LL BE IN THE HOUSE ALL THE TIME. IT'S JUST A BETTER ARRANGEMENT FOR ME.

AND FOR YOU—YOU GET TO BE INTIMATE WITH KINSEY. YOU GET A GIRL WHO WILL GIVE YOU WHAT YOU DESERVE. IT'S WHAT YOU WERE ALWAYS HOPING FOR.

WE'LL HAVE TO DO THIS QUICKLY. BODE IS UNCONSCIOUS NOW. WHEN BODE'S SPIRIT JUMPS OUT OF HIS BODY, I'M GOING TO DIVE STRAIGHT IN, BEFORE HE UNDERSTANDS WHAT'S HAPPENING.

DON'T WASTE TIME. YOU WANTED TO WEAR THIS SKIN.

IT'S ALL YOURS.

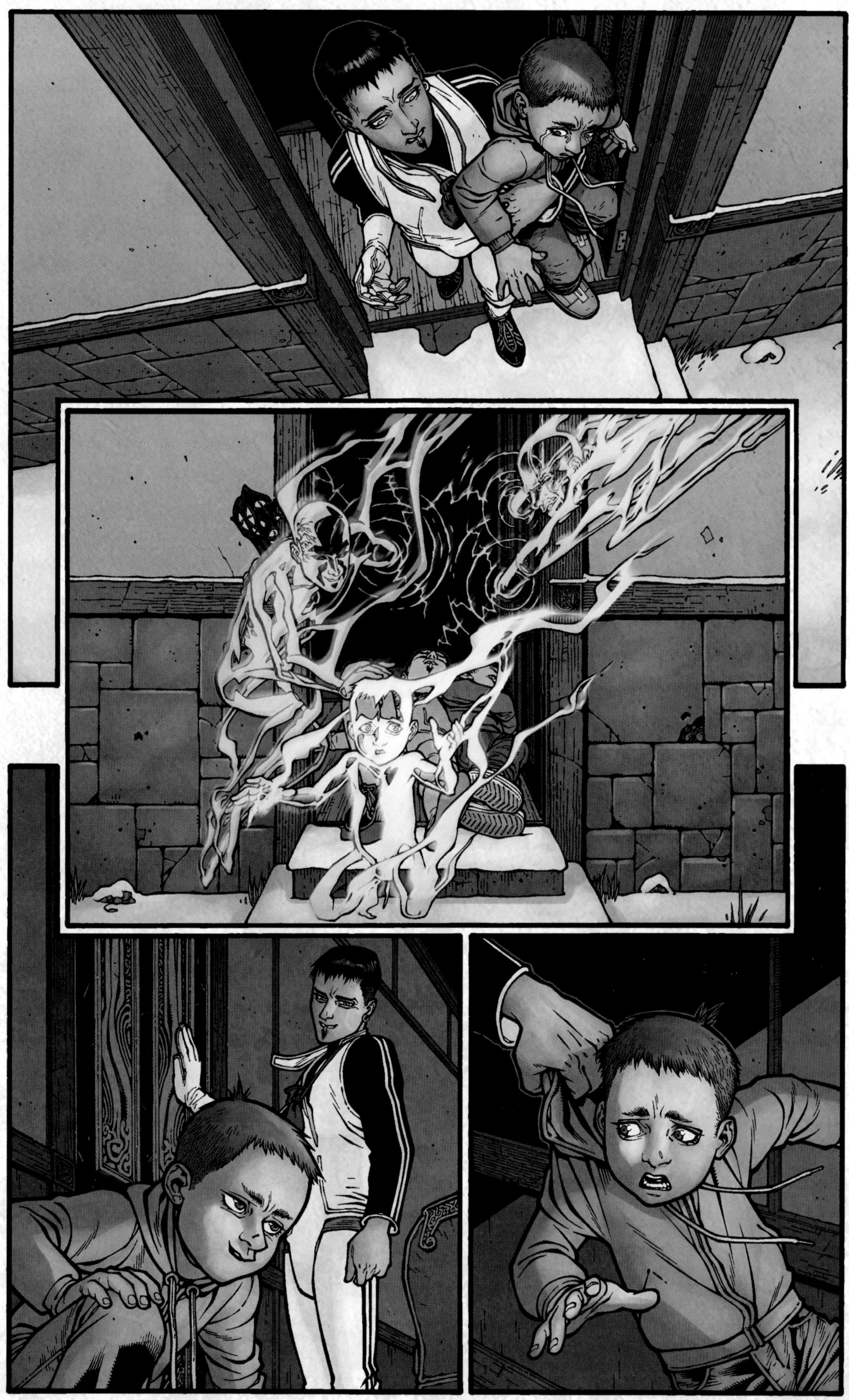

NO! DON'T! SAM, TAKE A MOMENT AND THINK ABOUT WHAT YOU'RE DOING!
I'VE HAD PLENTY OF TIME TO THINK ABOUT IT.
IT'S ALL I'VE THOUGHT ABOUT FOR MONTHS.
I'M GOING TO SEND YOU BACK TO OBLIVION. JUST LIKE I PROMISED. YOU TAUGHT ME THAT, DODGE. HOW IMPORTANT IT IS TO KEEP YOUR PROMISES.
NO! PLEASE! HELP!
WHAT THE FUCK? PENCILS? WHERE'S THE KEY TO THE WELLHOUSE? WHERE ARE ALL THE OTHER KEYS?
OH, PLEASE, SAM? HAVE I EVER NOT BEEN THREE STEPS AHEAD OF YOU?
I KNEW YOU'D COME BACK TO KEYHOUSE.

NUUUUH... PLUHH—!
I'M NOT AFRAID TO KILL YOU.
NO MORE TALK. JUST BE QUIET. I HAVE TO DO THIS.
YOU MADE ME DO THIS.
KINNNNMM MMA—NNG GAAA—
OH, TYLER! TYLER! I W-WUH-WAS S-S-SO... SO... SK-SCUH-SCARED...
HE'S DOWN! HE'S DOWN, JUST STOP!
I NEED TO BE SURE.
IT'S ALL RIGHT, LITTLE MAN. I'VE GOT YOU.

THAT'S IT. I HAVE NO RESPIRATION AND NO PULSE. I'M CALLING IT. NOTE THE TIME.
IS HE DEAD?
YEAH. DEAD BEFORE WE GOT HERE.
GOOD.
I SUSPECT A BLOOD SAMPLE WILL PLACE ZACK WELLS—IF THAT IS HIS NAME—AT THE SCENE OF JOE RIDGEWAY'S MURDER. WHICH PUTS HIM DOWN FOR TWO HOMICIDES WE CAN PROVE, PLUS—
I'M TAKING BODE INSIDE.
NOT YET, TYLER. HE NEEDS TO BE EXAMINED BY—
LOOKS LIKE YOU NEED A DOC MORE THAN HIM, MR. MUTUKU. BESIDES, IF SOMEONE WANTS TO EXAMINE HIM, THEY CAN DO IT INSIDE.
IN HIS BEDROOM. WHERE HE KNOWS HE'S SAFE. C'MON, KID. NO ONE IS EVER GONNA HURT YOU LIKE THAT AGAIN.
PROMISE?
PROMISE.

- KEYS TO THE KINGDOM -

The End

...to be continued in Locke & Key: CLOCKWORKS

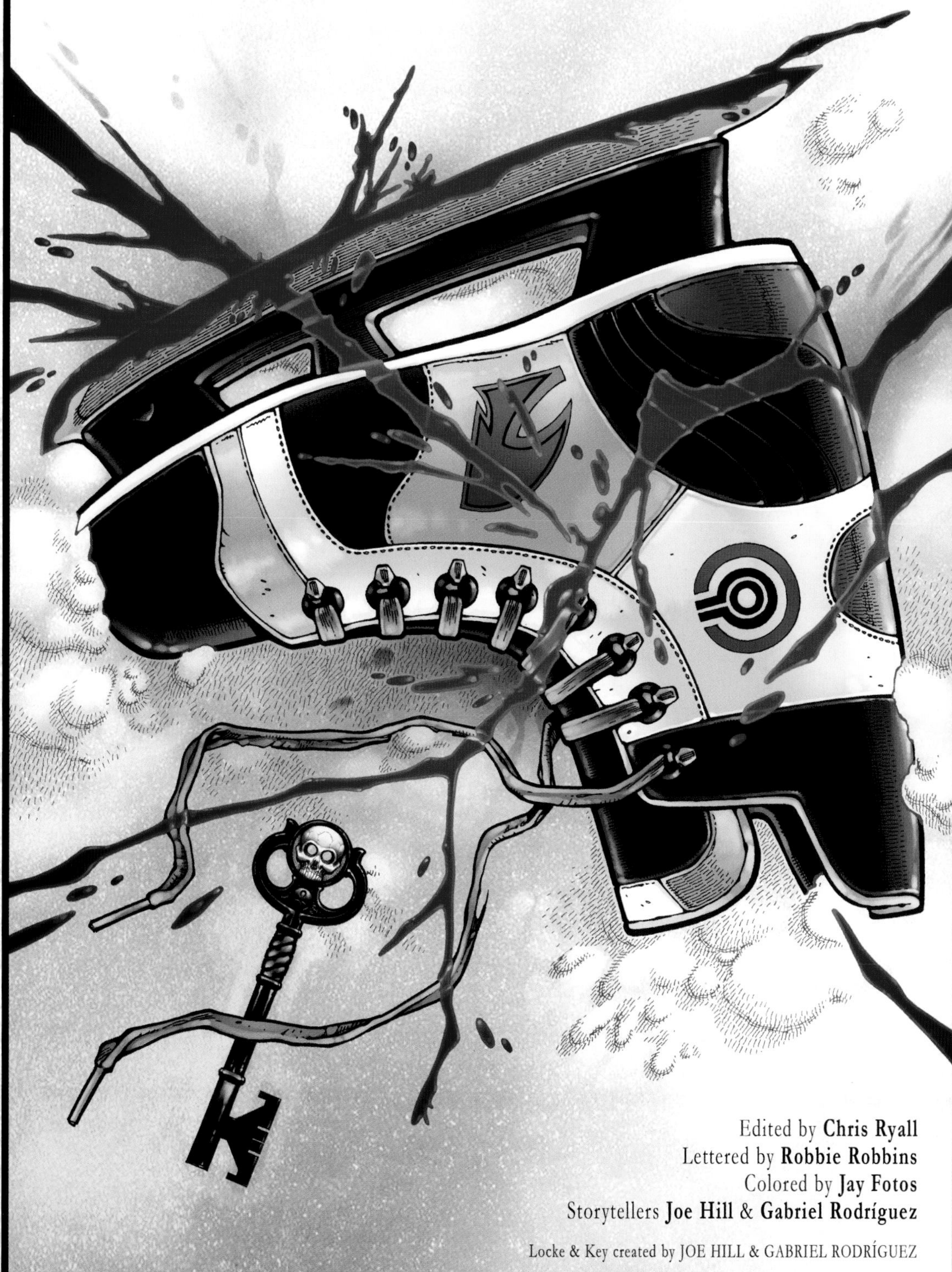

Edited by **Chris Ryall**
Lettered by **Robbie Robbins**
Colored by **Jay Fotos**
Storytellers **Joe Hill** & **Gabriel Rodríguez**

Locke & Key created by JOE HILL & GABRIEL RODRÍGUEZ

The Known Keys

(Excerpts from the diary of Benjamin Pierce Locke, 1757 - 1799)

ΩMeGa Key

in our
& I resolv
hazzarded such a
long I worked in a
till finallie t'was cas
oh how I feerd!
in the gathr
straiked o
held the d
beig'd
Gon
ho

GHoST KEY

onlee in occaisonull daith do I find peece now, for with the bode caste aisyde, it is possibull for one to know his own ETERNAIL SOULE. My spairt cannot leeve the grounds of Keyhowse, but heyre I walke laik an aingel! I aim everywhare and nowhare at once, from the tall's towair, to the deepst caves. It is hard to dreem thair could be any dore more terryble or wondairfulle than that wych dyvydes deth from lyfe, yet my expairances at the thraishold of the black dore have teach'd me thair are worse things than to dyye...

BL

eCHo KEY

whence I unlock'd the dore I heerd a voice that saimed to ecko from the well & it aisk'd me who I sot & I spake of my brother. No sooner had the words pass'd my lips thence he ROSE from the WELL like a spairt & yet was living flaish, allthohe had dyed in the Drowning Caves not 6 weeks beefor. He clasp'd me to his bosom & sayd why do ye look so unhappy to see me brother, but I wast in feer for my allmaighty SOUL & fled to the howse & pray'd thair to the LORD
But in that grait howse, an ecko of my voice was all the reeply I receiv'd

BL

aNYWHeRe KEY
us'd the key to anyplaice againe, to return to Boston, & gaither intelaigents for Crais. Tis an act of terryble wychcraift, but better I do it, than my sister, who is obssaissed with REVENGING herself upon the RED-COATS, for thair violence agin our faither & brother & belov'd maither. Aye, my dredd of beeing called to accomnt someday by SATAN HIMSELF is a trifling concern when maiched with my desyre to rid the worlde of the devylls who taik the King's Coyne to do raip & murdur...
BL
HeaD KEY
of alle the keys I have forged from the WHISP'RING IRON, 'tis the key that opens the human mind I most regrait. Miranda hast a pervairse fasinaytion whist the key & hast us'd ait to fill her head with all thair is to know about WAR & the SLAIYING of MEN, & she carrys an arsanall whist her whairever she goes. Yet I am less in dred of what she has put in than what she hast remov'd. Sometimes it is as if she is now without FEER and indeed is herself more man than I!
BL
GeNDeR KEY
my sister - or should I now say my brother! - fights the shadow war with Crais in the streets of Boston whilst I wait at home, like a helpless maiden, praying to the ALLMAIGHTY! for her safe return. When first I fashin'd the key, I imagained she maight trainsform to a boy to protect her, if necessaire, from the unsavorie lusts of ENGLISHMEN should the King's foot-soldiers return to Lovecraft to abuse God fairing womain. Never did I think she wouldst WILLENGLY caist off the wardrobe of her femininitie for this ruggaid liberation among men...
BL

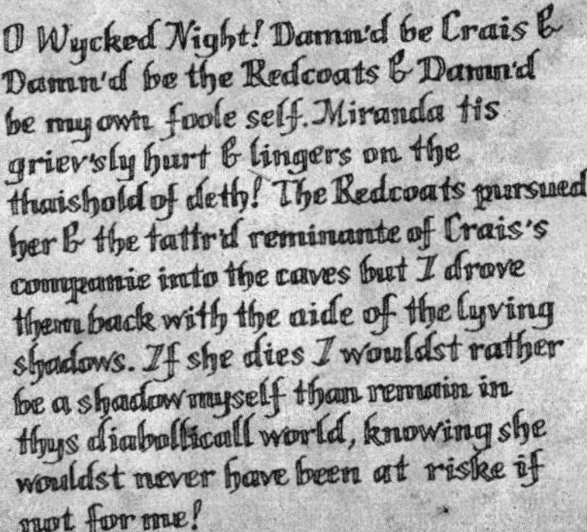

SHaDoW KEY

O Wycked Night! Damn'd be Crais & Damn'd be the Redcoats & Damn'd be my own foole self. Miranda tis griev'sly hurt & lingers on the thaishold of deth! The Redcoats pursued her & the tattr'd reminante of Crais's companie into the caves but I drove them back with the aide of the lyving shadows. If she dies I wouldst rather be a shadow myself than remain in thys diabollicall world, knowing she wouldst never have been at riske if not for me!

GiaNT KEY

she is dying & thair is nothing I can do to save her!
The Redcoats return'd to assalle the house & claym her & I admitte I lette my fury & miserie get the better of me. I used the giant's key to multiplie my syze, so that my body was as vaste as my hayte & I turn'd upon a wholle regiment & ~ O GOD forgive me! ~ did detestably murther them alle!

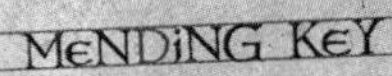

MENDiNG KEY

the Iron whispr'd to me laste night & I work'd in a fever alle day, mayking a cabinet & forging a new key out of that dreadfull metal that is not metal. Yet if the devil may pervairt Holie Scripture to serve his purposes, so may the rihteous at times turn the DEVYLLS TOOLS to do the work of SWEET JESU! For the key & cabinet I fashin'd could be used to mend fraicturd objykts ~ shatter'd plattes, crack'd eggs & broken sistairs. Bless'd be THE LORD, Miranda hast recovr'd! I only wish she wouldst remembair her place & become the demure & modestte girlle she once was, but fear her love for Crais will emperille her againe soon enough...

Animal Key

September 9th, 1851~

...Ulysses said he would fly all the way to Hell if he had to, to find Delacorte for me. Clint said he would probably only be required to fly to Georgia, but that the two places were much alike, except Georgia is a bit hotter. We have fought a thousand times, my brothers and I, but this morning I felt I could not love any living souls more. Ulysses stepped through the door, and emerged on the other side, a golden eagle. He gave me a short, lordly look, and took to the skies...

Music Box Key

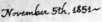

November 3rd, 1851~

...he was dying fast from his injuries and knew it. He said he would go to glory and take his secrets with him. Ulysses said that if our Lord meant to open the Gates Of Heaven to a B---- like him, he would prefer to throw in with the Devil. Clint hissed and seemed ready to strike again, but I restrained him. I knew if Hammersmith died, I would likely never see Delacorte again, and so I turned the Key in the Music Box, and the tune began to play. A miniature version of myself turned around and around, and sang:
...tell us who paid you for the girl...
...do it now before you leave this world...
Hammersmith's eyes widened, and he began to speak...

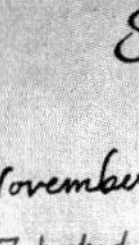

Skin Key

November 5th, 1851~

...I looked into the mirror, and turned it, so I became of the African race, and my skin was dark as coal. And it is a wonderment to me. All my thoughts had, until then, been bent on finding Delacorte and beseeching her to become free and white like myself. But when I saw my black features in the mirror, I was surprised to find I liked my own face better than I had ever liked it before. Ulysses considered me for the longest of times, before offering me my hat and saying: «Remember to keep your eyes down, Harland. You have the White Man's habit of meeting another man's gaze, but you will fare poorly if you behave that way here in Georgia.»

Engels-Schlüssel

4. Juni 1942

Mein Gott. Mein Gott! Bei Tagesanbruch war ich draußen und suchte nach dem kleinen Joe. Es stürmte und regnete in Strömen. Alles kam mir krank und unwirklich vor – wie in einem Albtraum. Ich rannte und rannte, völlig verzweifelt, und es war mir scheißegal, was er Jean über mich erzählte. Wenn en tot war, wollte ich selbst auch sterben. Und dann sah ich etwas Unglaubliches – etwas, das es gar nicht hätte geben dürfen, und ich bekam vor Überraschung und Staunen ganz weiche Knie. Ich sah Jean durch den Regen hinauffliegen, den zerschlagenen Körper ihres Bruders in der Armen. Sie trug das Gurtzeug mit den Flügeln, und hintendrin steckte der Schlüssel. Ich schwöre, sie ist geflogen! Und dabei sah sie so wunderschön aus wie eine Trauertaube.

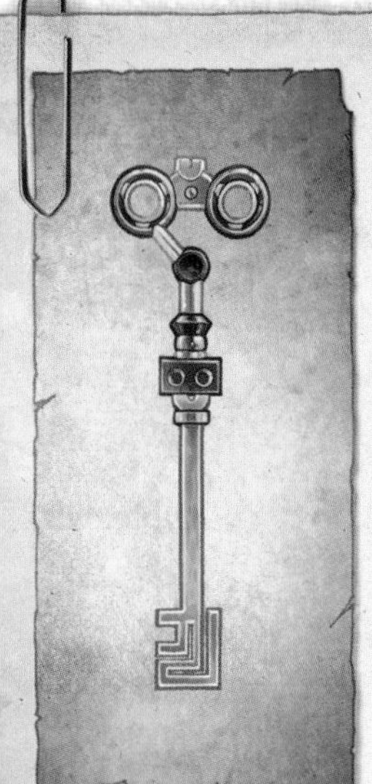

Philosophoscope Key

July 3rd, 1942

...Hannes asked me to come with him, in his quiet inflected English. I told him I liked it better when I thought he was mute because at least then he couldn't tell me lies. But I took his hand and went with him. He walked me to the Philosophoscope in the tower. Once I realized where we were going, Johnnie, I didn't want to go, and couldn't help myself. Once I realized what he was going to show me. He put the Key in, and shifted the lever to Truest Love and asked me to look. Oh Johnnie. How I have lied to myself for months. He knew what I would see somehow even when I didn't... that I would see him...

Herkules-Schlüssel

13. Juli 1942

Die Hälfte der 8. Armee und ein schier endloser Haufen SS-Männer warteten da auf mich! Ich schleuderte Eric gegen die Mauer und hörte, wie seine Rippen brachen, als wäre jemand auf ein Bündel Zweige gesprungen. Ich muss zugeben, das hörte sich wie Musik in meinen Ohren an!
Mit der anderen Hand schlug ich nach den Soldaten, und sie flogen wie Streichhölzer durch die Luft. Der Herkules-Schlüssel setzte all die Kraft in mir frei, die ich als verdammter Krüppel nie gehabt hatte. Aber der Sturmbannführer wusste, wie er mich fertigmachen konnte!